ISRAEL

THE INCONVENIENT TRUTH DIVIDING THE WORLD AND THE CHURCH

JAMES P SMITH

"One cannot and must not try to erase the past merely because it does not fit the present"
– Golda Meir

CONTENTS

INTRODUCTION

Barely a week goes by without Israel being in the news for some reason; rarely is that reason good and rarely does that reason paint Israel in a positive light. If you believed everything you hear and see on the news about Israel (and sadly most people do) you would be forgiven for believing that the Jews illegally occupy a land stolen from an indigenous Arab "Palestinian" people they are trying to exterminate in a way all too often compared to the Nazis' extermination of the Jews. For many, the image below is a justified representation of Israel's evil.

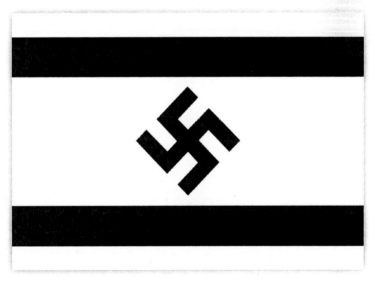

After all, the United Nations (UN) has condemned Israel time and time again, passing twice as many resolutions against Israel than all other states combined. In spite of Israel being the only true democracy in the Middle East, Israel is denied a seat on the UN Security Council, when even countries such as Syria and Zimbabwe have held seats. In fact, a 2003 European Union poll (published in *The Economist*) suggested that 59% of Europeans considered Israel to be a greater threat to world peace than Iran, North Korea and Pakistan. Is this really an accurate reflection of the true danger posed by Israel, the legitimacy of its claim on the land of Israel and its supposed mistreatment of the people known as Palestinian?

In providing an answer we must take an honest and objective look at the history of both the Jews and the Palestinians and the conflict between them. To do that, we need to start at the beginning.

The truth is an inconvenience to both the world and the church.

CHAPTER 1

ISRAEL: THE MAN, FAMILY, THE NATION

Israel's history is exceptionally ancient. It is recorded in the Old Testament and confirmed by archaeology and the non-Biblical texts of other ancient nations. For example, one of the oldest known non-Biblical references to Israel is found in the famous Merneptah Stele, an inscription by Merneptah, a pharaoh in ancient Egypt who reigned from 1213 to 1203 BC. It was discovered at Thebes in 1896 and is now displayed at the Egyptian Museum in Cairo (see Appendix 1 for more examples of how ancient non-Biblical sources confirm the Old Testament record of Israel's long history).

Abraham

The nation we know as Israel, the race of people called the Hebrews, or Jews, started with a man called Abraham, or Abram, as he was first known, the tenth generation from Noah through the line of Shem; Noah prophesied in Genesis 9:26 that God would bestow great blessing upon the line of Shem and Genesis 11:10-12:3 provides the genealogy of Shem through to Abraham, and the blessings given by God to Abraham and his descendants.

Abraham was born 352 years after the Flood, approximately 2,000 years before the birth of Christ. Abraham was the first man to be called a Hebrew, a name derived from Eber, an ancestor of Noah's son Shem. Shem is from where we get the term "semite", which historically has always been used to describe anyone of Middle Eastern origin, and yet "antisemite" is a term commonly used nowadays only in relation to the Jews.

While listed first among the three sons of Terah (Genesis 11:26), Abraham was not Terah's firstborn son. The Old Testament tells us that Terah was seventy years old when his first son was born and Abraham was born sixty years later when Terah was 130 years old (Genesis 11:32; 12:4). Abraham is listed as first among his father's sons because of his faithfulness to God and prominence in the history of the Hebrew nation, not because he was his father's firstborn son.

Genesis chapter 12 tells us how Abraham (then known as Abram) was chosen by God and called out of the land where he was living, which was in Ur of the Chaldees. Ur is one of the oldest recorded cities and its ruins are still visible today if you manage to travel to the edge of the al-Hajar Desert in modern-day Iraq. It was a centre for the cult worship of the moon god called Sin (rather appropriately).

God called out Abraham from his homeland with the promise of making him "into a great nation" (Genesis 12:2) with an unconditional covenant; the actual covenant ceremony is found in Genesis chapter 15, which clearly demonstrates the covenant is based on God's faithfulness, not Abraham's. Genesis 13:14-15 and Genesis 17:8 describe the giving of physical land to Abraham and his descendants "forever" as an "everlasting possession". Genesis 15:18-21 gives the specific and literal geographical dimensions of the land promised to Israel; an amount of land that Israel is yet to fully possess; it is a prophecy yet to be fulfilled completely, but without doubt Israel's regathering in 1948 as a literal nation again is a partial fulfilment of Biblical prophecy.

Isaac

Abraham had two sons, Ishmael born of Hagar and Isaac born of Sarah. God reaffirmed His covenant with Abraham's second son, Isaac:

> Sarah your wife shall bear you a son, and you shall call his name Isaac; I will establish My covenant with him for an everlasting covenant, and with his descendants after him (Genesis 17:19).

> But My covenant I will establish with Isaac, whom Sarah shall bear to you at this set time next year (Genesis 17:21).

Jacob

In the same way, God made clear that Jacob was the covenant child of Isaac, not Esau (Genesis 28:13-14). God identifies Himself in the Bible over thirty times as the God of Abraham, Isaac and Jacob.

Just as God renamed Abram, Abraham, so too God gave Jacob a new name, **Israel**. The twelve sons of Jacob became the 12 tribes of the nation of Israel and are commonly referred to as the "Children of Israel"; the nation that God promised to Abraham – the Hebrews. To be precise, Joseph became two tribes (Ephraim and Manasseh, with the tribe of Levi not being assigned specific land because of their role as the priestly tribe (Joshua 13:14, 33; 18:7).

1 Chronicles 16:15-17 confirms the everlasting covenant of land that God made with Abraham, Isaac and Jacob:

> Remember His covenant forever, the word which He commanded, for a thousand generations, the covenant which He made with Abraham, and His oath to Isaac, and confirmed it to Jacob for a statute, to Israel for an everlasting covenant.

And the Psalmist declares:

> He remembers His covenant forever, the word which He commanded, for a thousand generations, the covenant which He made with Abraham, and His oath to Isaac, and confirmed it to Jacob for a statute, to Israel as an everlasting covenant, saying, "To you I will give the land of Canaan as the allotment of your inheritance" (Psalm 105:8-11; see also Luke 1:54-55, 68-73).

Canaan

God promised Abraham and his descendants the land of Canaan and Genesis chapter 12 describes Abraham leaving his homeland and going to the land of Canaan, where "the Canaanites were in the land". The land of Israel was first known as Canaan, home to the Canaanites, part of the Hyksos people who gained control of northern Egypt most likely around 1650 to 1550 BC, ruling until they were expelled from Egypt around a century later by Ahmose I.

As part of the promise given to Abraham in Genesis 12:1-3, God declared:

> And in you all the families of the earth shall be blessed (v3).

For this blessing to happen, a descendant of Abraham was to come to prominence in the future. This particular individual was spoken of by Jacob, just before his death, when he blessed each of his sons. His special blessing was not for his first-born, but for his fourth son Judah, from whom we derive the term Jew. The tribe of Judah would provide the lineage for David, Solomon and eventually Jesus Christ, through whom all families of the earth shall be blessed. It was the tribe/nation of Israel that God would set apart and through it bring His own Son into the world (see Appendix 2 for detail of how Jesus fulfilled so many Old Testament prophecies).

CHAPTER 2

FROM ISRAEL TO PALESTINE

Jacob and his 12 sons were living in Canaan, just as Jacob's father Isaac had done before him. Things were far from harmonious within the family, with Jacob's favourable treatment of his youngest son, Joseph causing much resentment and jealousy between the other brothers. So much so that they sold him to slave traders, who took him to Egypt. However, as a result of God blessing and protecting Joseph there, he was ultimately appointed to a prominent position in Egyptian government, second only to Pharaoh.

As a result of a famine in the land of Canaan some time later, Jacob sent his sons to Egypt to buy much needed food. They were surprised (and initially horrified) to find their brother Joseph there, and in such a powerful position in Egyptian government. Bearing in mind their mistreatment of their younger brother, they understandably first feared Joseph would want revenge and kill them. However, Joseph invited his brothers to relocate their families to Egypt, so he could provide for them. Sure enough, Jacob, his sons and all their family members moved to the safety of Egypt (this whole account is covered in Genesis chapters 37 to 47).

Birth of a Nation

The Old Testament book of Exodus is the record of Israel's birth as a nation. It was within the protective "womb" of Egypt that the 70 family members that moved to Egypt steadily grew into a nation of several million people.

Over a period of around 400 years, the family of Jacob multiplied and prospered in Egypt. In fact, they became so numerous that the Egyptians enslaved them in fear of them taking over. So fearful were they that the Pharaoh commanded the midwives to kill at birth all the Hebrew male children (Exodus 1:15-16). It was into this perilous time that Moses was born. When Moses was grown, he was called by God to deliver the Israelites out of Egypt (Exodus chapter 3).

Instead of leading the Israelites directly to the land that God had promised them through Abraham, Moses led them to Mount Sinai. It was while they were encamped there that God gave Moses a set of legal codes. The Law of Moses became the new nation's constitution.

However, because they refused to trust and obey God, they spent the next 40 years wandering through the desert. It was Moses who led Israel out of Egypt and to the brink of the promised land but it was his successor, Joshua (Joshua 11:23) who led them into it.

The Israelites battled to take the promised land from the Canaanites, Hittites, Girgashites, Amorites, Perizzites, Hivites, Jebusites, Edomites, Moabites, Ammonites, Amalekites, Arameans and Philistines; more on the Philistines later.

After Joshua died, the Israelites spent the first several hundred years of life in their own land being ruled by a succession of judges appointed by God. The book of Judges names Israel's judges as Othniel, Ehud, Shamgar, Deborah, Gideon, Tola, Jair, Jephthah, Ibzan, Elon, Abdon and Samson. The book of 1 Samuel lists Eli the priest, Samuel the prophet, and Samuel's sons as leaders in this respect too (1 Samuel 4:18, 1 Samuel 7:15-8:3).

Saul was Israel's first king but it was their second king, David who was regarded as their greatest (as recorded in the Old Testament books of 1 and 2 Samuel and 1 and 2 Chronicles). One of David's most celebrated feats was capturing Jerusalem in around 1,000 BC and making it Israel's capital, from where he ruled Israel for 33 years; prior to making Jerusalem his capital, David ruled from Hebron for seven years (1 Kings 2:11).

Under David's son, Solomon, the kingdom of Israel is considered to have reached its zenith in wealth, power and magnificence. He built the first Jewish temple in Jerusalem in around 960 BC where the Israelites worshiped God according to the Laws of Moses. It also housed the Ark of the Covenant which contained the Ten Commandments.

Solomon was famous for his wisdom (1 Kings 4:29-34), but his son Rehoboam less so. In fact, his lack of wisdom led to the 10 tribes of northern Israel breaking away under the rule of Jeroboam (in around 931 BC). The 10 northern tribes became known as Israel and the two remaining southern tribes, Judah.

The northern kingdom of Israel was a disaster right from the start, with the condemning statement of "He did evil in the sight of the Lord" being used to describe all of its 19 kings. This is what led God to judge them by allowing Israel to be conquered.

Conquering Empires

In around 722 BC, Samaria, the capital of the 10 northern tribes of Israel was conquered by the Assyrian Empire and many Israelites were taken into captivity (2 Kings 17:5-6). Judah's independence lasted a little over a century longer but in around 597 BC it was conquered by the Babylonians, with many Jews taken back to Babylon; Jerusalem was laid siege to and eventually destroyed (along with the first temple) in 586 BC. Of the 19 kings and one queen of Judah, only eight did "what was right in the sight of the Lord". The others copied the sins of the kings of Israel.

Around 538 BC, the Persian Empire led by king Cyrus conquered the Babylonian Empire, including Jerusalem. In 516 BC, Cyrus issued a decree allowing the Jews in exile in Babylon to return to Jerusalem and rebuild the temple. Extra-Biblical records, such as the famous "Cyrus cylinder" from the ancient Persian empire (exhibited in the British Museum for all to see) confirm this as historical fact; an event that Isaiah prophesied would happen (Isaiah 44:28 – 45:1) over 200 years earlier, including the naming of Cyrus.

The land of Israel remained a Persian province until it was conquered yet again, this time by Greece in 332 BC under the leadership of Alexander the Great. Greek culture appealed to many Jews; the Greek translation of the Hebrew Bible (the Septuagint) was completed in the second century BC, and things went pretty well for the Jews under the rule of Antiochus III the Great. However, things went considerably less well under his son, Antiochus IV Epiphanes. He arrogantly gave himself the title of Epiphanes, which means "manifestation of a god". He initiated an all-out attack on Judaism and the banning of Jewish practices. This provoked a

Jewish revolt in 167BC that succeeded in regaining Jerusalem.

The revolt was first led by Mattathias of the priestly Hasmonean family and then by his son Judah the Maccabee. The revolt resulted in the Jews entering Jerusalem and purifying the temple (164 BC); events commemorated each year by the festival of Hanukkah.

Following further Hasmonean victories (147 BC), the Seleucids (a Greek royal family founded in 312 BC by the Macedonian general Seleucus I Nicator) restored autonomy to Judea (as the land of Israel was now known as). With the subsequent collapse of the Seleucid kingdom (129 BC), Jewish independence was again achieved. Under the Hasmonean dynasty, which lasted about 80 years, the kingdom regained boundaries not far short of Solomon's realm and political consolidation under Jewish rule was attained and Jewish life flourished.

All that changed when Roman General Pompey captured Jerusalem in 63 BC and the Romans deposed the ruling Hasmonean dynasty in 40 BC. The land of Israel became a province of the Roman Empire in 6 AD.

70 AD

Since Israel (or more accurately Judea as it was known then) had become a province of the Roman Empire, the Jews had not taken it lying down and had revolted against their Roman rulers several times. In 70 AD, after several years of fighting between the Jews and Romans, Titus (who would become Emperor) destroyed the temple in Jerusalem and burned the city, killing 1.1 million Jews (according to historian Josephus) and enslaving others by shipping them off to the gladiatorial games or Roman mines. However, the majority of the population was still allowed to remain in Israel. This was not a mistake the Romans would repeat.

135 AD

The final straw for the ruling Romans was the infamous Bar Kochba revolt of 135 AD. The revolt in fact started in 132 AD and was prompted by the actions of Emperor Hadrian, who during his travels through Judea in 130 AD indulged himself in several provocations, including decreeing a ban on circumcision, constructing a tomb to Pompey (who had desecrated the temple in Jerusalem in 63 AD) and pronouncing that he would rebuild Jerusalem as a Roman city and call it Aeolia Capitolina. The name Aelia came from Hadrian's family name, Aelius. The name Capitolina meant that the city was dedicated to the Capitoline Triad, a cult of Jupiter, Juno and Minerva. He also declared an intention to construct a temple to Jupiter Capitolinus on the site of Herod's temple.

Palestine

All these things stirred up the Jews who promptly revolted under the leadership of Simon Bar Kochba (whom many Jews believed to be their Messiah). The Romans prevailed and, in order to prevent any further uprisings, Emperor Hadrian banished the Jews from the land and renamed it Palaestina, from where we get the English term Palestine.

In actual fact, the full name given to the land of Israel by Hadrian was Syria Palaestina, which in Latin means "land of the Philistines". Hadrian tried to eradicate Jewish identity from the land of Israel by renaming it after its previous occupants, the Philistines. It is therefore vitally important to understand who the Philistines were, because it has been dishonestly and deceptively claimed they were a race of ancient Arabs from whom the Jews stole the land of Israel. For example, Minister of Religious Affairs for the Palestinian Authority, Mahmoud al-Habbash declared about the land of Israel:

> There was no period in history without the presence of the Palestinian people on this land.

This is complete fantasy and demonstrably so.

Philistine

The word "Palestine" is not an Arab word and is not found in the Arabic language. The letter "P" does not even exist in Arabic, so the word "Palestine" is so foreign to Arabs they cannot even pronounce it in their native tongue; they instead pronounce it "Filastin"; neither the word "Palestine" nor "Filastin" appears in the Qur'an; not even once.

The Philistines most certainly were **not** a race indigenous to Arabia; nor are the Arabs of today descended from the Philistines. Arabs are (by their own acknowledgement) descended from the firstborn of Abraham, Ishmael; for Arabs to be descended from the Philistine race, the Philistines would have to have been descended from Ishmael, but history clearly shows the Philistines were an established race of people long before Ishmael was even born. Genesis 10:13-14 tells us very clearly where the Philistines originated from:

> Mizraim begot Ludim, Anamim, Lehabim, Naphtuhim, Pathrusim, and Casluhim (from whom came the Philistines and Caphtorim).

The Philistines were in fact an Aegean (Mediterranean) people more closely related to the Greeks. Indeed, Amos 9:7 says the Philistines came from Caphtor, which is today identified as the Greek Island of Crete. Archaeological evidence supports this, with ceramic pots found in Israel where the Philistines lived being almost identical to pots unearthed on mainland Greece.

While the Philistines were an invading force and most certainly not indigenous to the region, it is clear that they had been in the region before Israel was established as a nation. For example, Genesis 21:32 describes how Abimelech and Phichol returned to the land of the Philistines after having made a covenant with Abraham. And Genesis 26:1 describes how Abraham's son, Isaac, went to Abimelech king of the Philistines, in Gerar, a Philistine town situated south of Gaza. Gerar is further referenced in 2 Chronicles 14:12-18 as being rich pastoral country.

Peleset

The Philistines were descended from one of the groups that made up the Sea Peoples from the Aegean known as the Peleset. The first known record of the Peleset is in ancient Egyptian inscriptions and texts; the most notable being the mortuary temple of Pharoah Rameses III at Thebes, part of which is translated as follows:

> · They were coming forward toward Egypt, while the flame was prepared before them. Their confederation was the **Peleset**, Tjekker, Shekelesh, Danuna, and Weshesh, lands united. They laid their hands upon the lands as far as the circuit of the earth, their hearts confident and trusting (emphasis added).

This recorded attack by the Sea Peoples mentions the Peleset as one of the conspirators along with other groups. Rameses claims he defeated them all in one battle on land and another at sea closer to Egypt known as the Battle of the Delta. There are also Egyptian reliefs of the battle that provide evidence of where the Peleset came from. For example, the reliefs depict the prow and stern of the Peleset ships being decorated with the heads of birds very similar to those found on ships from the Aegean during the same period.

Another source is the Papyrus Harris (named after a famous collector of papyrus documents called Anthony Charles Harris) that covers the entire reign of Pharoah Rameses III (currently held by the British Museum in London). It describes what happened in the aftermath of the Battle of the Delta. Part of it reads:

> I extended all the frontiers of Egypt and overthrew those who had attacked them from their lands. I slew the Denyen in their islands, while the Tjekker and the **Peleset** were made ashes. The Sherden and the Wesheh were made non-existent, captured altogether and brought in captivity to Egypt like the sands of the shore, I settled them in strongholds, bound in my name. Their military classes were as numerous as hundred-thousands. I assigned portions for them all with clothing and provisions from the treasuries and granaries every year (emphasis added).

Rameses finally settled many of these people in southwestern Canaan in return for the task of protecting Egypt's border with Asia. The Peleset were specifically given the cities of Ashkelon, Ashdod and Gaza and eventually also occupied Ekron and Gath. Together, these five cities became known to scholars as the Philistine pentapolis and both Joshua 13:3 and 1 Samuel 16:7 confirm these as being cities of the Philistines.

Based on the Aegean origins of the Philistines it is perhaps unsurprising that the first known derivative of the term "Palestine" used in literature is found in the writings of the 5th century Greek historian and traveller, Herodotus; he is known to have travelled to Egypt, where records of the Aegean origins of the Philistines would have aligned with the Greek history he would have been familiar with.

In his work called *Histories*, Herodotus referred to the land of Israel in Greek as "Palaistine", which was his way of expressing his affinity with his Aegean ancestors, the Philistines. At the time of him writing *Histories* the term Israel was not heavily in use in the area, because the 10 northern tribes known as the kingdom of Israel had been conquered by Assyria several centuries before. It is therefore hardly surprising that Herodotus did not use the term, Israel.

While Judah had been conquered by the Babylonians over a century before Herodotus wrote *Histories*, the name Judah continued to be used (eventually morphing into Judea as the kingdom re-emerged years later).

So, in renaming Israel as Syria Palaestina, the Romans did officially what Herodotus had done in his writings unofficially: try to erase the Jewish identity from the land by linking it with the Aegean Philistines, who were themselves not indigenous to the land and had all but died out as a race by the end of King David's reign.

Neither Hadrian nor Herodotus was referring to an indigenous **Arab** people. There was no Arab Palestinian nation, kingdom or empire.

Jewish Palestine

After the failed Bar Kochba revolt and subsequent scattering of the Jews from the land by the occupying Roman forces, the word Palestinian came to be understood to refer to anyone of any race or origin who lived between Jordan and the Mediterranean. They could have been Jew, Christian or Muslim (albeit several hundred years later for Muslims, since Islam was not created until early in the 7th century AD).

Over time, occupants of Palestine could have been Jew, Arab, Greek Orthodox, Syrian Catholic, or even Armenian. For example, under the Ottoman Empire from the beginning of the 16th century the term Palestine was used as a general term to describe the land south of Syria; it was not an official designation. In fact, many Ottomans and Arabs who lived in Palestine during this time period preferred to refer to the land not as Palestine, but as Southern Syria, because the name Palestine was still identified with Israel and the Jews. How could that be true if there was an indigenous Arab race of Palestinians? It could not. There was never an indigenous race of Arab Palestinians; no race, kingdom or empire.

Jews were happy to be identified as Palestinians. Just a few examples of this fact are as follows:

> In 1908, the World Zionist Organisation established a Palestine office in Jaffa.
>
> During World War II, 30,000 **Jewish** soldiers fought in the British Army under Montgomery under the banner of the Palestinian Brigade.
>
> The Palestinian Symphony Orchestra was **Jewish**.

Before being renamed the Jerusalem Post, the **Jewish** national newspaper was for many years called the Palestine Post.

Before being renamed Bank Leumi, the **Jewish** national bank was called the Anglo-Palestine Bank.

In a 1970 interview on Thames Television's *This Week* programme, Golda Meir, Israel's fourth Prime Minister between 1969 and 1974 said:

> I am a Palestinian. From 1921 to 1948, I carried a Palestinian passport.

The left-hand poster on the next page that has often been used to support anti-Israel propaganda, was in fact a Zionist advert promoting tourism to the Jewish homeland of Palestine.

The poster beside it on the right was created by the Palestine Foundation Fund (also known as the Jewish National Fund) that was founded in 1901 to encourage fund raising to **legally** buy land in Palestine to "assist in the foundation of a new community of free Jews engaged in active and peaceable industry."

Opposite is the *Larousse French Dictionary* from 1939, listing in the appendix all the then current flags of the world in alphabetical order. Notice the flag for Germany contained the Nazi swastika, demonstrating this was a pre-1945 publication. Now look at the flag for Palestine, which contains the Jewish Star of David, thus demonstrating widespread and accepted **Jewish** association with Palestine. There was no national Arab Palestinian nation (Islamic or otherwise).

After World War I, the name Palestine was applied more officially to the territory placed under British Mandate; this

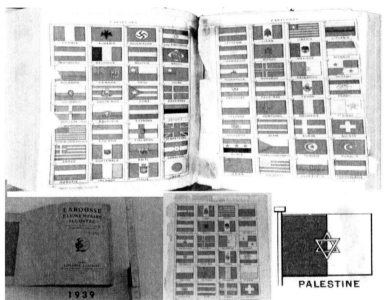

area included not only present-day Israel, but also present-day Jordan. Leading up to Israel's independence in 1948, it was common for the international press to label **Jews**, not

Arabs, as Palestinians living in the mandated area. What a short memory the world has!

This is all historical **fact** that is wilfully ignored and twisted by the Arab nations and replaced with a lie that is wholeheartedly believed by the West's politically correct secular news outlets.

Arab Palestine

So, I guess the next question is: How did the term "Palestinian" come to be used to describe only Arab Muslim people?

The origin of the modern-day understanding of a Palestinian was developed during the Cold War. Palestinian nationalism within Arabs was encouraged by the Soviet military and political advisers as a propaganda tool against Israel. This was because the fledgling nation of Israel (after World War II when Israel was again recognised as a nation in 1948) was seen by the Soviets as being an outpost of pro-western democracy in the Middle East and therefore a threat.

However, the current understanding of Palestine and who Palestinians are was only solidified as recently as the 1960s by the way the Soviets backed the Palestine Liberation Organisation (PLO), which was named by Yasser Arafat in 1964. Yasser Arafat was Egyptian, not Palestinian, and most of his PLO deputies were Tunisian Arabs (i.e. from North

Africa, not the Middle East).

The close relationship between the Soviets and Palestinian Arabs continued long after the 1960s, with recently uncovered documents showing that current Palestinian Authority President Mahmoud Abbas was an agent for the KGB in the 1980s. As reported on *SKY News* (8th September 2016), the documents proving Abbas' link to the KGB cannot be dismissed as Israeli propaganda, as the Palestinian Authority tries to claim, because they are Soviet era documents that were smuggled out of Russia by former KGB Archivist and Chief Directorate, Vasili Mitrokhin, who defected to the UK in 1992 following the collapse of the USSR in 1991. The documents were held at the Churchill Archives Centre at the University of Cambridge until they were made available for public research in 2014; Mitrokhin died in 2004 at the age of 81.

The PLO was committed to destroying Israel long before the 1967 Six-Day War, when Israel captured the Sinai Peninsula from Egypt, Judea and Samaria from Jordan (which was renamed the West Bank by Jordan), the Golan Heights from Syria, and seized control of (East) Jerusalem. It is therefore a total myth to suggest that the Arabs who today call themselves Palestinians are indigenous and the rightful owners of the land of Israel, and that the Jews are illegal occupiers; that is like claiming the Maori people occupy New Zealand! The Arab propaganda machine would have the world believe there were Palestinian Arabs in the West Bank **before** 1967, when in fact the West Bank was already **illegally** occupied by Jordan.

The West Bank

In April 1950, Jordan annexed East Jerusalem, Judea and Samaria and renamed those areas the West Bank and declared it a forbidden area for Jews. It never belonged to them; it was an illegal act, but only Britain (which had the mandate over the area) and Pakistan recognised it as such; 70% of the population in Jordan today is Palestinian Arab.

It is worth noting that you will never hear Judea, Judah or Samaria referred to by the western news outlets nowadays, as they have happily continued to use the name given to the area by the Jordanians who took it illegally – the West Bank. The western news outlets are no less guilty than the Romans were for trying to erase Jewish identity and history from Israel, and for allowing the Arabs to do this without question (to be very precise Judea was the region lived in by the tribe of Judah, the fourth eldest son of Jacob, but Judea and Judah have been used interchangeably down through history to describe the part of Israel that is now referred to as the West Bank).

When Christians in particular discuss the issue of who the West Bank belongs to, they should carefully read Ezekiel chapter 36. It begins, "And you, son of man, prophesy to the mountains of Israel, hear the word of the LORD!" and then goes on to describe how the Jews will come home to them, where towns will be inhabited and ruins rebuilt, and God will give the Jews the mountains of Israel as their inheritance. So, where exactly are the "mountains of Israel"? It is the very region of Israel that was offered to the Arabs in 1947 by the UN but rejected; the land known as Judea and Samaria – the West Bank. The most controversial area in the Middle East is the very place earmarked by God as an area of Jewish immigration. Christians at the very least should realise that the conflict over the land is **spiritual**.

The Jewish villages in this area are called yishuvim, meaning "settlement". To the outside world these Jewish villages are regarded as settlements in "occupied territory", thus giving them the distinct impression of being illegal. In reality, the Jews in the yishuvim are merely living out God's promise in Ezekiel chapter 36.

Denying History

In his book, *Why I Left Jihad*, Bethlehem born Arab, Walid Shoebat describes the notion of a Palestinian people as "a fiction of the Islamists" (page 27). He should certainly know, because before giving his life to Christ he was an active Palestinian terrorist.

Even ignoring the Biblical promises of the land from God to the Jews, the Jews can make a strong legal argument for being the genuine indigenous and historical inhabitants of the land called Israel, simply based on the archaeological evidence. Islam can make no such claim. Islam can only make a claim on the land based on religion, whereby if Muslims conquer a land, it is regarded as holy land and must therefore be theirs forever. Based on that faulty premise Islam still owns Spain!

Centuries of Jewish history is confirmed by historical accounts in the Bible and archaeological discoveries showing that the Jewish people lived in Israel, spoke the Hebrew language and worshipped the God of Israel for over a thousand years before the birth of Christ. In spite of the undeniable historical evidence (some of which is referenced in Appendix 1), on numerous occasions when archaeological finds have uncovered Jewish artefacts containing ancient Jewish symbols and Hebrew texts giving clear evidence of Jewish history in the land of Israel, the Palestinian Authority has told Arab Palestinians that the finds have been fabricated by the Israelis. For example, when Israeli archaeologists in 2013 displayed gold artefacts containing Jewish symbols (such as a menorah and a shofar) that were uncovered fifty metres from the Western Wall in Jerusalem, former Palestinian Authority Prime Minister Ahmed Qurei denied their authenticity. On

11th September 2013 he declared on official Palestinian Authority TV:

> I think all this is a forgery, forgery of the truth. It's all an attempt to make claims. They did not find anything.

Current Palestinian Authority leader Mahmoud Abbas is no better. On official Palestinian Authority TV on 17th January 2014, he described Jewish history in Jerusalem as a "delusional myth" and claimed that Israel is trying to invent a Jewish history "by brute force". In another talk he described Jewish history in Jerusalem as "illusions and legends" and even referred to the Jewish temple in Jerusalem as the "alleged temple", a term the Palestinian Authority regularly uses to deny it ever existed. In reality, the Arabs specifically built the Dome of the Rock in 691 AD to try and prevent the Jews from ever building another temple again (please see Appendix 1 for irrefutable evidence of Israel's history, confirmed by non-Biblical sources).

Both the Old and New Testament is set in the land of Israel; the word Palestine **never** appears in the Bible (nor in the Qur'an), whereas the word Israel occurs over 2,200 times in the Old Testament and 87 times in the New Testament. In spite of modern attempts at revising Biblical history to describe Jesus as the "first Palestinian martyr"[1], the land of Israel was not renamed Palestine (Syria Palaestina) until a century **after** the life of Jesus on earth. The New Testament presents Jesus as a Jew living in the land of Israel and the Jewish Messiah to the Jewish people; the Son of God sent to redeem us from our sins as prophesied by Isaiah and other Hebrew prophets. The Jewish identity of Jesus is made plain within the New Testament Gospels, not least at His crucifixion when the Roman authorities nailed Him to a cross under a sign that called Him "King of the Jews". Jesus identified Himself as a Jew. For example, when speaking with the Samaritan woman in John chapter 24, Jesus says:

> You worship what you do not know; we know what we worship, for salvation is of the Jews.   ·

Jesus celebrated Jewish festivals such as Passover and the Feast of Unleavened Bread (Luke chapter 22) and Hannukah (John chapter 10), which is not even specifically ordained in the Old Testament, thus demonstrating Jesus was completely immersed in Jewish culture and tradition. To claim He was a Palestinian is simply deranged fantasy at best and deliberately deceitful at worst.

If you listened to modern-day commentators, whose ignorant but loud opinion is based on Arab propaganda and lies, you would be forgiven for thinking that the Jews illegally stole Palestine from an indigenous Arab Palestinian people, who were fully occupying a cultivated and developed land.

There is still quite a bit of history to get through before the Muslims made their claim to Israel, sorry, Palestine, and the eventual rebirth of Israel in 1948.

CHAPTER 3

FROM PALESTINE TO ISRAEL

While most Jews were scattered abroad after 135 AD, there has **never** been a time when Palestine did not have a Jewish presence living in the land. For example, there was a continuous Jewish community living in Hebron from the time of the Babylonian exile in the sixth century BC, until the British expelled them in 1929 (after Arabs had rioted, murdered more than 60 Jewish men, women and children and looted Jewish homes and business). Other Jewish communities thrived for many centuries in places like Tiberius and Safed in the Galilee.

Islamic Expansion

It was not until the late seventh century AD, after the death of Mohammed that Arab Muslim armies waged war across the Middle East in the name of Islamic domination. They named the land Jund Filastin (meaning "the military district of Palestine") and built the Dome of the Rock and al-Aqsa Mosque on the place where Soloman's temple once stood; the gold plating to the dome was not added until the 20th century.

After the rapid expansion of Islam over the following few centuries, Muslims leaders were required to work out a way of dealing with non-Muslims, who remained in the majority in many areas for centuries. The solution was to develop the notion of the "dhimma," or "protected person" which applied to the "People of the Book" (how the Qur'an describes Christians and Jews). Though not forced to convert, the dhimmi were, in the best of times, second-class citizens and, at certain times and places severely persecuted and murdered. Christians were forced to wear blue to identify them and Jews yellow.

In a brazen attempt at rewriting history, some Islamic scholars claim the Jews were treated kindly by their Muslim conquerors, with Muslims and Jews living in peace together until the rise of the Zionist Movement of the 20th century. This is demonstrable nonsense. For example, consider the important Jewish philosopher, Moses Maimonides (1138 - 1204 AD), also known as Rambam (an acronym for Rabbi Moses ben Maimon). He was the first person to gather together all the Rabbinic Jewish law into one place, the Mishnah Torah. In his *Epistle to Yemen* (written around 1172 AD), he wrote:

> Remember my co-religionists, that on account of the vast number of sins, God has hurled us in the midst of this people, the Arabs [note he does not describe them as "Palestinians"], who have persecuted us severely, and passed baneful and discriminatory legislation against us, as Scripture has forewarned us, "Our enemies themselves shall judge us" [Deuteronomy 32:31]. Never did a nation molest, degrade, debase and hate us as much as they.

Note the distinction between Kedar and the children

of Ishmael, for the Madman [referring to Mohammed] and imbecile is of the lineage of the children of Kedar as they readily admit. Daniel alludes only to our humiliation and degradation "like the dust in threshing" suffered at the hands of the Arabs [again, no mention of "Palestinians"], may they speedily be vanquished.

Similarly our sages instructed us to bear the prevarications and preposterousness of Ishmael in silence.

No matter how much we suffer and elect to remain at peace with them, they stir up strife and sedition, as David predicted, "I am all peace, but when I speak, they are for war" [referencing Psalm 120:7].

Does this sound like Maimonides thought Jews had it good under Muslim rule?

Does it sound like Muslims were treating the Jews kindly?

Far from it. Maimonides in fact makes the point that no matter how much the Jews tried to live in peace with the Muslim Arabs, the Muslims always wanted war and strife instead; nothing has changed over the last millennia.

First Crusade

Muslim rule continued until the taking of Jerusalem in 1099 AD by the Catholic Crusaders, three years after it began in 1096 AD. The First Crusade was precipitated by the following declaration by Pope Urban II in September 1096 AD:

Anyone who sets out on a journey, not out of lust for worldly advantage but only for the salvation of his soul and for the liberation of the Church, is remitted in entirety all penance for his sins, if he has made a true and perfect act of confession (*Chronicles of the Crusades*, page 60).

This promise of eternal reward for participating in "holy war" at the behest of Pope Urban II has no basis in the Word of God, but does sound alarmingly similar to the promise made in the Qur'an:

> And whether you die or are killed, unto Allah you will be gathered (Sura 3:158).

Second Crusade

The Second Crusade began in 1147 AD and lasted two years and was launched in response to the loss in 1146 AD of the Crusader principality of Edessa in ancient Mesopotamia to Muslim attackers. Pope Eugene III called for a new crusade to recover lost territory; not unlike the way in which Islam calls for lost territory to be regained and re-established as the House of Islam (Dar al-Islam) by military means. Pope Eugene III repeated Pope Urban II in erroneously connecting salvation to participation in his crusade:

> We enjoin you in the name of the Lord and for the remissions of your sins… that the faithful of God, and above all the most powerful and the nobles act vigorously to oppose the multitude of the infidel… and strive to liberate from their hands the many thousands of our brethren who are captives… We accord them that same remission of sins that our predecessor Pope Urban instituted (*The Crusades,* c.1071 – c.1291, pages 156-157).

Third Crusade

The Third Crusade lasted from 1189 AD to 1192 AD and was launched after the fall of Jerusalem to the renowned Muslim warrior Saladin (Salah al-Din) on 2nd October 1187 AD. Pope Gregory VIII called for a crusade on 29th October 1187 AD in very similar terms to the calls of his papal predecessors. The crusade army captured some land, including Acre in northwest Israel in July 1191 AD after a two year siege, but not Jerusalem, which was to remain under Muslim control for over seven hundred years.

The loss of Jerusalem led to an increase in the frequency of subsequent crusades. In 1198 AD, following in the footsteps of his predecessors, Pope Innocent III issued a call for a crusade to consolidate territory held in the Holy Land by offering remission of sin to anyone who would fight for his cause:

> All those who take the Cross and remain for one year in the service of God in the army, shall obtain remission of any sins they have committed, provided

they have confessed them (*Chronicles of the Crusades*, page 29).

Fourth Crusade

The resulting Fourth Crusade commenced in 1202 AD and lasted two years. However, political intrigue and internal power struggles led to this crusade taking an unexpected turn in which the crusading knights directed their aggression not against Muslim adversaries, but against the eastern part of the Roman Empire (known as the Byzantine Empire); the western part of the Roman Empire became suspicious that the eastern part was compromising with Muslims, so Constantinople was attacked and captured and a western ruler was put on the Byzantine throne.

The crusades came to an end in 1291 AD with the fall of Acre, followed by the loss of the last remaining coastal towns. The weakening of the eastern Roman Empire through the capture of Constantinople by the western Roman Empire directly led to the eastern Empire finally falling in 1453 AD to Ottoman Sultan Mehmet II; subsequent western Popes did not have the strength to take back the eastern empire from Muslim control.

Some Muslims (and non-Muslims for that matter) point to the atrocities committed during the Middle East Crusades as an example of "Christian" violence, but these people have not done their homework, because the crusades were Catholic, at the behest of unregenerate and evil Popes, who persecuted and murdered Christians and whose actions completely contradicted Christ's commands. Jesus said, "If you love Me, keep My commandments" (John 14:15), and "If anyone loves Me, he will keep My word" (John 14:23). Those who love and follow Jesus obey His commands, but those who claim to know Jesus yet do not obey His commands, are liars and the truth is not in them (1 John 2:4). It must be said that the Popes responsible for the military crusades did not keep Christ's commands; they did not love Jesus, nor did they know Him, and in fact the number of Muslims killed by the Roman Catholic Popes is tiny compared to the millions of Bible-believing Christians murdered by the Popes; proof enough that the Roman Catholic Popes did not (and still do not) represent Jesus Christ.

Mamluks

In 1291 AD, the Crusaders were defeated by the Mamluks. The term Mamluk means "slave" in Arabic, and comes from the root malaka, meaning "to possess." The Mamluks were non-Muslim slave soldiers, mainly Qipchak (Kipchak) Turks from Central Asia, forced to convert to Islam by their masters. However, they finally realised the considerable power they had gained and rebelled against their Muslim masters and started their own dynasty based in Egypt.

Once they had gained control of Israel from the Crusaders, the Mamluks destroyed all the port cities, such as Jaffa and Caesarea in order to prevent the Crusaders from returning. However, their eventual defeat came not from the sea, but from the north from the expanding Ottoman Empire.

Ottoman Empire

From the early sixteenth century, Palestine was ruled by the Ottoman Empire.

The Ottoman Empire reached its zenith under Suleiman, who ruled from 1520 until his death in 1566; he was the longest-reigning Sultan of the Ottoman Empire. He made

Constantinople (now known as Istanbul) his capital.

Under his administration, the Ottoman Empire ruled an estimated 15-25 million people and stretched from Hungary to the Persian Gulf; from the Horn of Africa to the Crimean Peninsula. However, by the nineteenth century it was in deep decline, riddled with corruption and had become dependent on trade with European powers such as France, Germany, Russia and Great Britain. This economic dependence allowed European countries to assert influence and power over the treatment of non-Turkish, non-Muslim citizens within the Ottoman empire, who were regarded by the majority Muslim community as second-class citizens ("dhimmis").

19th Century

In 1839, Britain started diplomatic relations with the Turks and was the first western nation to open a consulate in Jerusalem, which was specifically set up for the protection of the Jewish people which, by the 1840s, was the largest single ethnic group in Jerusalem; a fact regularly ignored.

For many years during the nineteenth century, the British Consulate was located adjacent to the first protestant church to be established the Middle East. Today, what was the Consul's residence is now the Christ's Church rectory in Jerusalem. It was where in 1865 the Palestine Exploration Fund established its Middle East headquarters, with Queen Victoria as patron and the Archbishop of Canterbury as president.

Palestine was at the time a poor country, ruled by absentee Turkish landlords and largely barren and uninhabited. What population did exist outside the walls of Jerusalem consisted of mainly nomadic tribes. Thanks to the Turks, the land had been totally neglected. Hundreds of years of abuse had turned the country into a treeless waste, with malaria-ridden swamps, a few towns and a desert in the south too harsh to support human existence. These are incontestable facts regarding the state of the land in the late 19th Century that can be supported by **independent** witnesses. Here are just a few:

Independent Witness One - Sir John William Dawson

In 1888, Sir John William Dawson (1820-1899), a Canadian Geologist and university administrator, wrote of the area in *Modern Science in Bible Lands*:

No national union and no national spirit has prevailed there. The motley impoverished tribes, which have occupied it have held it as mere tenants at will, temporary land owners, evidently waiting for those entitled to the permanent possession of the soil.

Independent Witness Two - Alphonse de Lamartine

In Recollections of the East Volume 1, Alphonse de Lamartine (1790-1869), a French writer, poet and politician, wrote in 1835:

Outside the gates of Jerusalem we saw no living object, heard no living sound, we found the same void, the same silence…

Bearing in mind how historically

holy to Islam Jerusalem is claimed to be, and how it is claimed that an indigenous Arab nation already existed and thrived in Palestine, why did Alphonse de Lamartine find "no living object" outside the gates of Jerusalem? Were they all shy and hiding?

Independent Witness Three - Mark Twain

 Mark Twain; real name Samuel Langhorne Clemens (1835-1910), author of *Tom Sawyer* and *Huckleberry Finn*, witnessed the land for himself in 1867 during a tour of Europe and the Middle East that was sponsored by a local newspaper. He wrote a popular collection of travel letters, which were later compiled as a book, *The Innocents Abroad*. In one such letter in his book he made the following observation:

Of all the lands there are for dismal scenery, I think Palestine must be the prince… It is a hopeless, dreary, heart-broken land… Palestine sits in sackcloth and ashes. Over it broods the spell of a curse that has withered its fields and fettered its energies…

Nazareth is forlorn; about that ford of Jordan where the hosts of Israel entered the promised land with songs of rejoicing, one finds only a squalid camp of fantastic Bedouins of the desert; Jericho the accursed, lies a moldering ruin, today, even as Joshua's miracle left it more than three thousand years ago…

Renowned Jerusalem itself, the stateliest name in history, has lost all its ancient grandeur, and is become a pauper village... Capernaum is a shapeless ruin; Magdala is the home of beggared Arabs [note he does not refer to them as Palestinians]; Bethsaida and Chorazin have vanished from the earth... Palestine is desolate and unlovely. And why should it be otherwise? Can the curse of the Deity beautify a land?

There are of course many, many Jewish witnesses to the state of their homeland prior to 1948 and the re-emergence of national Israel. For example, in his book, *The Rediscovery of the Holy Land in the Nineteenth Century*, Yehoshua Ben-Ariah describes Israel at the time as "a derelict province" and "a sad backwater of a crumbling [Ottoman] empire" (page 11).

It is clear from the aforementioned first-hand accounts that there was absolutely no flourishing indigenous Arab Palestinian nation with a historical right to the land of Israel, living and thriving on a cultivated and well-farmed land. In 1838, Lord Shaftesbury expressed his hope that the land "when dug and harrowed" would provide "the testimony of the authenticity of the Bible"[2].

In 1863, British Consul, James Finn, conducted a census of the inhabitants of Jerusalem itself. The figures were published the following year and confirmed that of a total population of 15,000, 8,000 were Jewish, with the other 7,000 made up of a combination of Muslim and Christian (meaning neither Jewish nor Muslim). While wider Palestine remained largely uninhabited, Jerusalem had a **majority** Jewish population, even in the 19th century.

In the mid-nineteenth century, Sir Moses Montefiore was

given permission to purchase land outside the city walls of Jerusalem to pave the way for the expansion of the city of Jerusalem.

An Arab nation known as Palestine did not exist. The Jews living there at that time had not stolen the land from an indigenous Palestinian people. They had legitimately, legally and peaceably purchased the land from the absent and disinterested Turkish landlords; often at exorbitant prices.

Arab Immigration into Palestine

The truth is that most ethnic Arabs living in Israel/Palestine today are the children and grandchildren of Arabs who entered the land **illegally after** World War I, under the British Mandate (from Egypt - to escape heavy taxes, Transjordan, Syria and Lebanon to name but a few). Between 1922 and 1931, when the country was administered by the British, illegal Arab immigrants (i.e. extra to the agreed quotas) comprised of almost 12% of the Arab population. The *Hope Simpson Report* acknowledged in 1930 that there was an "uncontrolled influx of illegal immigrants from Egypt, Transjordan and Syria." The rate of immigration into Palestine increased even further during the 1930s. The Syrian Governor of Hauran admitted in 1934 that between 30,000 and 36,000 people from his district alone had entered Palestine that year and settled there; hardly indigenous.

In 1939, Winston Churchill said:

> Far from being persecuted, the Arabs have crowded in to the country and multiplied until their population has increased more than even all world Jewry could lift up [increase] the Jewish population.

This is a telling statement from Churchill, because it makes plain that rather than there being an indigenous Palestinian

people, the occupants of the land had "crowded in" from other countries. The **Jews** are the **indigenous** people of the land of Israel.

Jewish Immigration into Palestine

In the 1880s, there was an increase in the number of Jews migrating to Palestine who were fleeing persecution and massacre in Russia (known as the pogroms). Increasing antisemitism across Europe birthed the Zionist Movement, led by Theodor Herzl. The aim was to bring about a formally recognised Jewish state in Palestine, where Jews would be safe from persecution and attack. Although Herzl never lived to see his dream fulfilled, the First World War brought about the beginning of its realisation. At the same time, an Arab nationalist movement in the crumbling Ottoman Empire began to emerge; Arabs against the Turks; this had nothing to do with Arab Palestinian nationalism.

20th Century

At the outbreak of the First World War in 1914 the Turkish Ottoman Empire made the mistake of siding with the Austro-Hungarian Empire and Germany against France, Russia and the British Empire. Great Britain, together with allies from Australia, New Zealand and across the British Empire fought against the Turks, who were backed by the Germans. As the war on the eastern front progressed both the British and French governments started to consider how the Ottoman Empire would be divided up in the event of its defeat.

In 1915, the British High Commissioner in Egypt, Sir Henry McMahon entered into official correspondence with Husain bin Ali, the Sharif (noble) of Mecca. These private letters involved commitment from the British to support independence for the Arab states that were under Ottoman rule, but with the explicit **exclusion** of the region known as Palestine. Not only was this explicitly outlined in McMahon's letters to the Sharif of Mecca but also in correspondence he wrote to others. For example, in a letter to John Shuckburgh in 1922 describing the nature of his correspondence with the Sharif of Mecca, he wrote, "It was fully my intention to exclude Palestine". In 1937 McMahon wrote a letter to *The Times* in which he wrote:

> I felt it my duty to state, and do so definitely and emphatically, that it was not intended by me in giving this pledge to King Hussein to include Palestine in the area in which Arab independence was promised. I also had every reason to believe at the time that the fact that Palestine was not included in my pledge was well understood by King Hussein.

Notice how McMahon made reference to Arabs, rather than Palestinians. Why? Because, as we have already established, there was no Arab Palestinian state, nation or kingdom.

Sykes-Picot Agreement

In 1916, a secret geo-political agreement was drawn up between the British, French and Russians for carving up a defeated Ottoman Empire into French and British administered areas, including Turkish-held Syria, Lebanon and Palestine; it was devised as a partition not between Jews and Arabs but between what the British and the French would govern. This agreement became known as the Sykes-Picot Agreement, named after its chief negotiators, Sir Mark Sykes and Francois Georges Picot.

By the time the Ottoman Empire did collapse, the Sykes-Picot Agreement was rendered irrelevant due to an upsurge of nationalism in the area, the rise of modern Turkey and the Bolshevik revolution that turned Russia from an ally to an enemy of France and Britain.

While the agreement never had any power in international law, it did nevertheless have an impact and influence on the subsequent San Remo Agreement that replaced it in respect of the initial demarcation of Lebanon, Iraq and Palestine borders; the San Remo Agreement that followed did have power in international law, ratified by all members of the League of Nations (the forerunner to the United Nations).

In late 1916, the allied forces, known as the Egyptian Expeditionary Force, were nearing the Egyptian city of Al-Arish and the border with Palestine, thus ensuring a sufficient buffer zone against further Turkish and German aggression against the strategically vital Suez Canal. By this time, David Lloyd George had replaced H. H. Askwith as the British Prime Minister and Lord Arthur Balfour had been appointed Foreign Secretary. Both men were determined to liberate the land of Palestine from the Turks and protect it from further invasion (or from being split) by either the Turks or Germans.

In Britian, consideration for the aspirations of the Zionist Movement led to the government's Balfour Declaration.

Balfour Declaration

On the 31st October 1917, as the war cabinet met in Whitehall to decide on the final wording for what would become known as the Balfour Declaration, unbeknown to them at the time, the allied forces had won their first victory in the campaign to liberate Palestine from Turkish control. Earlier that day, the British and New Zealand forces had paved the way for Australian forces on horseback to take the historic town of Beersheba (first named by Abraham after he made a covenant with king Abimelech of Gerar - Genesis chapter 21:22-34).

The taking of Beersheba was vital to the allied forces securing the Sinai Peninsula and ensure the shipping corridors along the Suez Canal.

News of the victory in Beersheba reached London on 2nd November 1917; the same day of Lord Balfour's letter to Lord Rothchild. The letter stated:

> His majesty's government view with favour the establishment in Palestine of a national home for the Jewish people, and will use their best endeavours to facilitate the achievement of this object, it being clearly understood that nothing shall be done which may prejudice the civil and religious rights of existing non-Jewish communities in Palestine, or the rights and political status enjoyed by Jews in any other country.

Notice the declaration makes **no** reference to a Palestinian people. It refers to Jews and non-Jewish communities but not a Palestinian people. Why? Because there was no recognised Palestinian race of people, let alone an existing Palestinian nation in the land.

The victory at Beersheba quickly paved the way for the conquest of Jerusalem, thus bringing it under British rule. It was General Sir Edmund Allenby who led the allied forces into Jerusalem on 11th December 1917. General Allenby famously commanded his soldiers to dismount and enter Jerusalem on foot through the Jaffa Gate in recognition of Jerusalem's status as a holy city.

A year later on 1st October 1918 the Turkish Ottoman Empire surrendered to the allies, with the Armistice of Mudros signed on 30th October. Surrender of the Germans and Austro-Hungarian Empire followed shortly after.

Paris Peace Conference

The First World War ended in November 1918 and a peace conference took place in Paris in early 1919. The Balfour Declaration had the full support of the allied powers and was a pledge to facilitate the formation of a Jewish national home in Palestine. Crucially, and contrary to popular belief today, the Balfour Declaration also had support from Arab leaders at the time. In January 1919 Chaim Weizman, the leader of the Zionist Organisation met with one of the sons of the Sharif of Mecca, the Emir Faisal of the Arab kingdom of Hejaz (on the west coast of the Arabian Peninsula). Their discussions resulted in the signing of an agreement on 3rd January 1919 that made clear the territory of Palestine was to be for the Jews. In fact, the third article of the agreement specifically refers to the Balfour Declaration in respect to Palestine. Part of the agreement states:

> Mindful of the racial kinship and ancient bonds existing between the Arabs and the Jewish people, and realising that the surest means of working out the

consummation of their national aspirations is through the closest possible collaboration in the development of the Arab State and Palestine, and being desirous further of confirming the good understanding which exists between them.

Again, notice how the agreement refers to Jews and Arabs, not Palestinians.

While the opening of the Paris Peace Conference took place at the French Foreign Ministry in Paris, later sessions were held at the Palace of Versailles, which resulted in the famous Treaty of Versailles being signed on 28th June 1919 that became legally binding for the nations of Europe that took part in the First World War. Not only did it formally end the war, but also dealt with the territories previously ruled by the former Ottoman Empire. The Supreme Council of Allied Powers invited both Arab and Jewish representatives to present their territorial claims.

On 6th February 1919 the Arab delegation presented its claim. An Arab representative at the Paris Peace Conference declared:

> We will push the Zionists into the sea, or they will send us back to the desert.

As part of the Paris Peace Conference, the King–Crane Commission was appointed at the request of American President Woodrow Wilson. Speaking at the King-Crane Commission, Arab leader Aref Basha al-Dajani ominously warned:

> It is impossible for us to make an understanding with them [the Jews] or even to live them together...

Their history and all their past proves that it is impossible to live with them. In all the countries where they are at present they are not wanted and are undesirables, because they always arrive to suck the blood of everybody, and to become economically and financially victorious. If the League of Nations will not listen to the appeal of the Arabs this country will become a river of blood.

The British delegation at the conference was represented by Prime Minister David Lloyd George and Lord Balfour. The Arab representative, Emir Faisal specified the Arabs wanted to establish independent states. What is very important to note is that in describing the territory where the Arabs would have autonomy and independence, Emir Faisal left out Palestine, thus honouring the agreement he and Chaim Weizman had signed on 3rd January 1919 and acknowledging that Palestine was not to be part of the new independent Arab states.

Three weeks later, on the 27th February 1919, Chaim Weizman of the Zionist Organisation presented their claim and in doing so specified the scope of the territory they were asking for. They presented a map of Palestine showing where the new Jewish state would be situated both east and west of the Jordan River; all areas of both historical and Biblical significance to the Jews; all land allotted to the twelve tribes of Israel as recorded in the Old Testament several thousand years before. The decision was adjourned until after the League of Nations had been constituted, which also happened at the Paris Peace Conference.

Prior to the First World War, a state conquering another state in a legitimate war had the right of annexation (a formal act whereby a state proclaims its sovereignty over territory previously outside its domain). Many countries had expanded their power and influence by doing this through setting up colonial governments in a conquered country while maintaining sovereignty to itself. However, at the end of the First World War, as a result of opposition from American President, Woodrow Wilson, (who believed the war should bring to an end the practice of annexation of conquered land and be replaced by the self-determination of peoples) Britian and France were unable to annex the parts of the Ottoman Empire they had conquered. The mandate system was therefore created as a compromise between America and Britain and France.

Jan Christian Smuts was one of the founding members of the League of Nations and a co-author of the covenant of the league. He was also a member of the war cabinet that decided on the final wording of the Balfour Declaration on the 31st October 1917; there is a statue of him in London standing opposite the Houses of Parliament. The mandate system originated from Article 22 of the covenant, in which one country is entrusted with the administration of another country not yet ready for self-government. Therefore, with the full agreement of the League of Nations, Britain was given the mandate over Palestine. It had the full backing of Woodrow Wilson, who saw the newly formed mandate system as a way of guaranteeing self-determination of peoples; the first time international law recognised this right.

Under the mandate system, in recognition of their historical links to the land, the Jewish people were chosen to be beneficiaries of a mandate held by the British government in respect of Palestine. Likewise, the Arab inhabitants of Mesopotamia (Iraq) were chosen to be the beneficiaries of a mandate held by the British and Syria and Lebanon held by the French.

San Remo Conference

The Supreme Council of Allied Powers that met at the Villa Devachan in San Remo, Italy in April 1920 was made up of five nations: Great Britain, America, France, Italy and Japan. The British delegation was led by Prime Minister David Lloyd George.

From a legal perspective, San Remo was responsible for turning the promise of the Balfour Declaration of 1917 into a legally binding agreement in international law.

While discussing what land should be allocated for the creation of a Jewish state, David Lloyd George referred to a specific map created by renowned geographer and expert in the Middle East, George Adam Smith, which maps the kingdoms of David and Solomon. It was a recognition the Jews had an historical connection to the land going back several thousand years. The minutes of the meeting held on the 25th April 1920 made clear that what was to be given to the Jews was not just a small piece of Palestine, but all the land covered on George Adam Smith's map of the ancient kingdoms of David and Solomon.

The San Remo Resolution of April 1920 was later unanimously endorsed by all 51 countries of the League of Nations, thus giving it full international recognition in law. It was a watershed moment in the history of the Jewish people who had been exiled from their national homeland for almost 2,000 years. Referring to the San Remo Resolution, Chaim Weizman, who would later become the first president of

Israel, told the Zionist Annual Conference in July 1920:

> Recognition of our rights in Palestine is embodied in the Treaty with Turkey, and has become part of international law. This is the most momentous political event in the whole history of our movement, and it is, perhaps, no exaggeration to say in the whole history of our people since exile.

The Zionist Organisation of America responded similarly by stating:

> The San Remo decision of the Supreme Council of the Peace Conference crowns the British [Balfour] Declaration by enacting it as part of the law of the nations of the world. Upon Great Britain has been conferred that mandate which gives to it and to its people the high privilege of translating the promise of the British [Balfour] Declaration into high fulfilment. Deep and unshakable is our faith in the good will of Great Britain, so to observe the terms of the mandate as shall make of Palestine at the earliest possible moment a home for numbers of our people waiting to be admitted.

The minutes from the San Remo Conference were discovered in the British National Archives in the 1980s. Based directly on these documents, international lawyer, Howard Grief authored a book titled, *The Legal Foundation and Borders of Israel in International Law*. These documents make clear that the intended outcome of the Balfour Declaration on which the San Remo Resolution was built was a full Jewish state of Israel. Minute 12 of the war cabinet meeting on 31st October 1917 confirms this, which is important to note, because the

British government later denied it.

Palestine Mandate

Winston Churchill played a prominent role in the Mandate of Palestine. He was appointed Colonial Secretary in 1921, which gave him the responsibility of implementing the mandates in the former Ottoman Empire. Churchill visited Palestine in March 1921 and received a delegation from Arabs living in Palestine whose 35 page protest against Zionist activity included a variety of antisemitic tropes: "The Jew is clannish and unneighbourly. He will enjoy the privileges and benefits of a country but will give nothing in return." Churchill rejected their claims and made his government's position clear by stating:

> It is manifestly right that the Jews should have a National Home where some of them may be reunited. And where else could that be but in this land of Palestine, with which for more than 3,000 years they have been intimately and profoundly associated.

Churchill told the Jewish delegation which followed:

> The cause of Zionism is one which carries with it much that is good for the whole world, and not only for the Jewish people; it will bring prosperity and advancement for the Arab population.

Notice Churchill said it would bring prosperity and advancement not to an existing Palestinian nation but "for the Arab population". There was no recognised Palestinian state or nation, just Arabs living in Palestine.

On his return to London, Churchill told the House of Commons:

Anyone who has seen the work of the Jewish colonies will be struck by the enormous productive results which they have achieved from the most inhospitable soil.

The subsequent 1922 White Paper attributed to Churchill reflected his discussions with the Arabs and Jews the previous year and contained a phrase that was central to the assertion that the Jews "were in Palestine as of right and not sufferance". It was the Jew's right to return to their ancient homeland and was recognised as such in international law; they were not being given land that they had not previously owned.

In 1921, Faisal, whose father was supposed to be given rule of Syria was in disagreement over Syria with the French, who held the mandate over it. He was consoled by the British with the throne of British-controlled Mesopotamia (today's Iraq). But his brother Abdullah, vowing revenge against the French, led a force of his Bedouin followers from the Hejaz into the semi-anarchic area east of the Jordan. The British feared that a clash between Abdullah and the French might provide a pretext for the French, now their bitter rivals for dominance in the Near East, to implant themselves in that area. French rule over Transjordan would upset the Sykes-Picot treaty by cutting off British-controlled Mesopotamia from Palestine.

In order to avoid this, Churchill made a deal with Abdullah whereby, in return for promising not to attack the French in Syria, Abdullah was installed as Emir of Transjordan under the effective supervision of British advisers. The British Mandate for Palestine was expanded eastwards to embrace Transjordan, with the proviso that the clauses of the draft mandate allowing for the establishment of a Jewish national homeland under British protection should not apply east of the Jordan. The arrangement was enshrined in the Churchill White Paper (policy statement) of 1922, debated and approved by British Parliament in the July of 1922 and the draft for the Mandate for Palestine was confirmed by the Council of the League of Nations on 24th July 1922. The mandate document was based so closely on the earlier Balfour Declaration that the preamble to the document incorporated the exact wording of the Balfour Declaration that made clear the mandate was created in order to reconstitute the Jewish homeland on its ancient and historic land. A foundational clause in the document states:

> Whereas recognition has hereby been given to the historical connection of the Jewish people with Palestine and to the grounds for reconstituting their national home in that country.

The Balfour Declaration, San Remo Resolution and Churchill's White Paper that became the Mandate for Palestine, all formally recognised the cultural historic roots of the Jewish people to their ancient homeland and their right to return there. They acknowledged a pre-existing legal right of the Jewish people and not the creation of a new right. This was acknowledged by not only the British government, but also the League of Nations (the forerunner to the United Nations).

Article 2 of the mandate states:

> The Mandatory shall be responsible for placing the country under such political administration and economic conditions as will secure the establishment of the Jewish national home.

The Mandate of Palestine was specific about who was the beneficiary of this right of self-determination, with a number of provisions to guarantee it, including the way in which the British authorities should cooperate with the Jews in running the mandate, encourage and facilitate the acquisition of citizenship by Jews and the immigration of Jews back to their homeland. The whole purpose of the mandate was for the Jews to be given the right to immigrate to the land in order for the population to increase to the point where they could declare independence and self-determination of their country. The mandate did not name any other ethnic group or peoples other than the Jewish people in respect of political rights to govern. It mentions the civil and religious rights of "non-Jewish" communities but not political; the mandate does not make reference to Arabs, let alone Palestinians.

These points about the explicit intention and purpose of the Balfour Declaration, San Remo Resolution and Churchill's White Paper that became the Mandate for Palestine are important, because the MacDonald White Paper of 1939 reneged on this by declaring that it was "not part of [the British government's] policy that Palestine should become a Jewish state". In spite of this being a demonstrable lie and the League of Nations Commission declaring the MacDonald White Paper was in conflict with the mandate, the British government nevertheless sought to limit Jewish immigration to Palestine and restricted Arab land sales to Jews.

In fulfilment of the agreement signed on 3rd January 1919 between Chaim Weizman and Emir Faisal, there were by 1922 three mandates in place for the purpose of forming four Arab nations; all of which successfully gained independence and selfdetermination by 1946. In spite of this, however, the

Arabs reneged on their part of the agreement in respect of the Jews and Palestine, with riots and uprisings against the Jews. A man called Haj Amin al-Husseini was central to this.

Haj Amin al-Husseini

Haj Amin al-Husseini (1895-1974) was a Muslim from Jerusalem, born into one of the ruling families under the Turkish Ottoman Empire. He was the uncle of Yaser Arafat, no less. Arafat's father was Abdul al Qudwa (or Kidwa). His mother was Hamida Khalifa Al-Husseini, one of the many cousins of Haj Amin al Husseini.

As a boy he attended Islamic, Ottoman and Catholic schools. He went to a French Catholic School in Jerusalem to learn the French language. While at the school he came into contact with priests and teachers who filled his impressionable mind with lies and conspiracies about the Jews.

When the First World War started, he joined the Turkish Army to fight for Turkey against the allied forces. He got injured during that time. At the end of the war, he moved his allegiance to the British in order to be on the winning side.

Nebi Musa Riots

In April 1920, al-Husseini called on Arabs from nearby towns and villages to converge on Jerusalem and wage jihad on the Jews.

Local Arab journalist, Aref al-Aref (who went on to become Mayor of East Jerusalem in the 1950s) incited the mob by declaring, "If we do not use force against the Zionists and against the Jews, we will never be rid of them". The angry Arab mob famously (or perhaps infamously would be more appropriate) shouted back, "We will drink the blood of the Jews" as they surged through the Jewish quarter and into West Jerusalem, venting their rage against any Jew they could find, burning and looting homes and shops, and even attacking British and Arab policemen.

After several days of rioting, six Jews had been killed, hundreds more beaten and multiple Jewish homes and shops had been destroyed. What became known as the Nebi Musa Riot was the opening salvo in a 90 year war waged by the Arabs to reverse the Balfour Declaration.

Haj Amin al-Husseini was sentenced to ten years' imprisonment by a British military tribunal for incitement of the Nebi Musa riots of 1920 but avoided jail by fleeing to Syria. He returned to Jerusalem after being subsequently pardoned shortly after by the British. In an attempt to appease the rioting Arabs, the British made al-Husseini the Grand Mufti (Islamic religious leader) of Jerusalem in 1921. It did nothing of the sort and merely gave al-Husseini a stronger footing from which to radically oppose British rule in Palestine and the creation of a Jewish homeland.

He then became the Chairman of the Palestinian Muslim Council and, in 1928 he created the Supreme Muslim Council. He travelled the Middle East gaining considerable influence, spreading rumours throughout the Arab world about a Zionist plot to destroy the Muslim holy sites in Jerusalem. Put plainly, Haj Amin al-Husseini hated the Jews.

Anti-Jewish violence erupted in Jerusalem again in August 1929 as a direct result of al-Husseini inciting the Arabs with fallacious claims that the demand of the Jews for access to the wall (the holiest place for orthodox Jews) threatened the very existence of the al-Aqsa and Dome of the Rock. On 23rd August, Arab crowds marched into the orthodox Jewish quarter of Jerusalem and initiated a wave of violence that left both Jews and Arabs dead.

In 1931, he called together in Jerusalem the World Islamic Council, at which he announced a boycott of trade with any Jew in Palestine and the Middle East.

In 1933, as a result of contact instigated by Haj Amin al-Husseini only months after Hitler had become Chancellor of Germany, Nazi leaders travelled from Germany to Jerusalem to meet with him to commence talks on how Muslims and Nazis could work together in the Middle East against both the British and the Jews. In a telegram sent back to Berlin on 31st March, the German General Consul in Jerusalem, Heinrich Wolff, reported on his meeting with Husseini:

> The Mufti explained to me today at length that Muslims both within Palestine and without welcome the new regime in Germany and hope for the spread of fascist, anti-democratic forms of government to other countries. Current Jewish economic and

political influence is harmful everywhere and has to be combated. In order to be able to hit the standard of living of Jews, Muslims are hoping for Germany to declare a boycott [of "Jewish" goods], which they would then enthusiastically join throughout the Muslim world.

In 1937, eleven years before the re-emergence of the state of Israel, al-Husseini published a booklet called "Islam and the Jews", regarded by many as the founding document of Islamic antisemitism. He went back to the 7th century and Mohammed's war against the Jews and linked this with the war he believed that all Muslims must fight against the Jews. For example:

> The battle between Jews and Islam began when Mohammed fled from Mecca to Medina…In those days the Jewish methods were exactly the same as they are today. Then as now, slander was their weapon. They said Mohammed was a swindler…They tried to undermine his honour…They began to pose senseless and unanswerable questions to Mohammed…and then they tried to annihilate the Muslims. Just as the Jews were able to betray Mohammed, so they will betray the Muslims today…the verses of the Koran and the Hadith assert that the Jews were Islam's most bitter enemy and moreover try to destroy it.

The influence of this booklet on the increasing Arab hatred of the Jews in the early part of the 20th century **before** Israel becoming a nation again cannot be overstated; Muslim antisemitism was in existence and growing long before Israel became a nation again.

In the same year, evading an arrest warrant, al-Husseini fled Palestine and took refuge first in the French Mandate of Lebanon and then the Kingdom of Iraq, where – with the help of German Nazis - he joined with Muslim soldiers to create a coup in order to rise up and make the nation of Iraq radically anti-British, anti-Jewish and pro-Nazi. His coup failed and, under the protection of the Italians, he fled first to Italy and then from there to Berlin a month later in October 1941, which is where he met Adolph Hitler face-to-face for the first time. He first met with German foreign minister Joachim von Ribbentrop in Berlin on 20th November and then with Hitler himself one week later, on 28th November 1941.

Meeting the Fuhrer

During the meeting, al-Husseini assured Hitler that: "The Arabs were Germany's natural friends because they had the same enemies as had Germany, namely the English, the Jews and the Communists", and that "they were prepared to cooperate with Germany with all their hearts". He said the Arabs "could be more useful to Germany as allies than might be apparent at first glance, both for geographical reasons and because of the suffering inflicted upon them by the English and the Jews." Hitler in return confirmed that "Germany stood for uncompromising war against the Jews", including "active opposition to the Jewish national home in Palestine". He assured al-Husseini that:

> Germany was resolved, step by step, to ask one European nation after the other to solve its Jewish problem, and at the proper time to direct a similar appeal to non-European nations as well.

We of course know what Hitler's **final solution** was to the "Jewish problem".

As recorded in the minutes of the meeting, Hitler urged his guest to remain patient:

> At some not yet precisely known, but in any case not very distant point in time, the German armies will reach the southern edge of the Caucasus. As soon as this is the case, the Fuhrer will himself give the Arab world his assurance that the hour of liberation has arrived. At this point, the sole German aim will be the destruction of the Jews living in the Arab space under the protection of British power.

Notice how Hitler referred to "Arab space", rather than Palestinian space. Why? Because, as we have established several times, there was no formal Palestinian state. There were simply Muslim Arabs living in Palestine.

In the same meeting, Hitler also assured al-Husseini of his opposition to the establishment of a Jewish national homeland in Palestine, which, he said, "would be nothing other than a political base for the destructive influence of Jewish interests." More than 15 years earlier, Hitler had expressed the same thought in more colourful terms in Mein Kampf:

> They are not at all thinking of building a Jewish state in Palestine in order, for instance, to live there; but rather they only hope to have a headquarters for their international swindling operations that is furnished with sovereign powers and removed from the influence of other states.

At their meeting, Hitler and al-Husseini solidified their plans to destroy the British and the Jews. It was agreed that al-Husseini would use Berlin as his base from which he would promote the annihilation of the Jews to the Muslim world; the plan was for Hitler to annihilate the Jews in Europe and al-Husseini would do the same in the Middle East.

Such was the influence of al-Husseini that in a speech to the World Zionist Congress in Jerusalem on 20th October 2015, the Israeli prime minister Benjamin Netanyahu described him as "inspiring the Holocaust" and urging Hitler to exterminate the Jewish people.

Radio Propaganda

From 1939 to March 1945, the Nazi regime broadcast radio propaganda every day from the outskirts of Berlin via (what was at the time) one of the most powerful shortwave radio transmitters in the world, for the purpose of reaching Arabs and Muslims in the Middle East and North Africa with Nazi propaganda. It appealed to the Muslim world by suggesting Islam and National Socialism had shared political interests and goals and ideological passions, including hatred of the Jews. Haj Amin al-Husseini was central to all this and spoke himself on the radio broadcasts from Berlin. For example, on 7th July 1942, nearly six years before Israel became a nation again, al-Husseini broadcast the following message:

> According to the Muslim religion the defence of your life is a duty which can only be fulfilled by annihilating the Jews. Kill the Jews, burn their property, destroy their stores, annihilate these base supporters of British imperialism. Your sole hope of salvation lies in annihilating the Jews before they annihilate you.

And in a separate radio address in 1942, he declared:

> Kill the Jews – kill them with your hands, kill them with your teeth. This is well pleasing to Allah.

On 1st March 1944, in response to support in the United States Congress for a Jewish homeland in Palestine, al-Husseini made the following statement in Arabic in a Berlin radio broadcast:

> The wicked American intentions toward the Arabs are now clearer, and there remains no doubt that they are endeavouring to establish a Jewish empire in the Arab world. More than 400,000,000 Arabs oppose this criminal American involvement... Arabs! Rise as one and fight for your sacred rights. Kill the Jews wherever you find them. This pleases God, history and religion. This serves your honour, God is with you.

Radios were not common in the Arab world at the time but it was Mussolini who shipped in 90,000 radios and set them up in cafes, markets and other key public places in order to ensure the propaganda reached the widest possible audience. It grew to having an estimated one million listeners every week. Haj Amin al-Husseini broadcast similar messages from Rome, Italy for Mussolini. For example, al-Husseini broadcast a message from Rome warning that:

> If the invasion is not repelled, the Jews will establish their national home not only in Syria, Lebanon and Transjordan and Egypt, but also throughout all the neighbouring Arab countries. The Arabs must struggle against the British and the Jews, the deadliest enemies to Islam, shoulder to shoulder with the Axis.

The radio messages always started with long readings from the Qur'an by Arabic speakers who had been trained by Hitler's chief propandist, Joseph Goebbels, which were then intertwined with conspiracy theories about how evil the Jews were and their plans to take over the world. Through the radio broadcasts al-Husseini's speeches and essays of the 1930s and 1940s reached hundreds of thousands of Muslim listeners, as well as being distributed in thousands of print editions. For example, in July 1942, 200,000 leaflets were flown to North Africa with an appeal by al-Husseini for Muslims to join the Nazi cause.

The relentless radio addresses and leaflet drops encouraged thousands of Muslims across the Middle East and Africa to fight on the side of the Nazis in the belief they shared the same goals and same common enemy. Their role and influence on today's antisemitism in Palestinian and Arab politics cannot be underestimated.

Among his other activities in Berlin, Haj Amin al-Husseini served as honorary chair of the newly founded Islamic Central Institute, which was officially opened on 18th December 1942, during Eid al-Adha, the Islamic Festival of Sacrifice. In a letter to Hitler to mark the occasion, al-Husseini expressed the hope that "thousands of Muslims around the world" would cooperate with Germany in the fight against "the common enemies": "Jews, Bolsheviks and Anglo-Saxons." Having been approved by German Minister of Foreign Affairs, Joachim von Ribbentrop, the opening address was given by al-Husseini and was broadcast all across North Africa and the Middle East. It showed he needed no lessons from the Nazis in his hatred of the Jews. He called for all Muslims to rise up against the Jews and their allies. He declared:

> The Jews and their accomplices are to be counted among the bitterest enemies of the Muslims, who made known … their hostility since ancient times and have everywhere and always … treated them [Muslims] with guile.

> Every Muslim knows all too well how the Jews afflicted him and his faith in the first days of Islam and what hatefulness they displayed toward the great Prophet — what hardship and trouble they caused him, how many intrigues they launched, how many conspiracies against him they brought about —such that the Qur'an judged them to be the most irreconcilable enemies of the Muslims …

> They will always remain a divisive element in the world: an element that is committed to devising schemes, provoking wars and playing peoples off against one another …

In England as in America, it is the Jewish influence alone that rules; and it is the same Jewish influence that is behind godless Communism …

And it is also this Jewish influence that has incited the nations into this gruelling war. It is only the Jews who benefit from the tragic fate that they [the nations] suffer …

In a subsequent talk at the Islamic Central Institute on 2nd November 1943, he called on Muslims to follow the example of National Socialist Germany, since it "knew how to save itself from the evil done by the Jews... It had precisely identified the Jews and decided to find a definitive solution to the Jewish menace, in order to eliminate their evildoing from the world." Many have pointed to such comments made by Haj Amin al-Husseini as evidence that he was well informed and supportive of the Nazi extermination programme that was by this time long underway in the Nazi death camps in occupied Poland; he was certainly given tours of the Nazi

concentration camps and given the honour of inspecting German troops.

In fact, even after 1943 when it was beginning to dawn on the Nazi regime that Germany would likely lose the war, al-Husseini made repeated efforts to ensure that no European Jews managed to avoid the death camps. For example, Bulgarian plans to permit some 4,000 Jewish children and 500 adult companions to immigrate to Palestine provoked a letter from him to the Bulgarian foreign minister, pleading for the operation to be stopped. In the letter, dated 6th May 1943, al-Husseini wrote:

> I would like to call your attention to the fact that it would be very appropriate and more advantageous to prevent the Jews from emigrating from your country and instead to send them where they will be placed under strict control: e.g. to Poland. Thus one can avoid the danger they represent and do a good deed vis-à-vis the Arab peoples that will be appreciated.

One week later, he sent additional letters to both the Italian and German Foreign Ministries, appealing for them to intervene in the matter. The German Foreign Ministry promptly sent a cable to the German ambassador in Sofia stressing "the common German-Arab interest in preventing the rescue operation." Indeed, according to the post-War recollections of a Foreign Ministry official, "The Mufti turned up all over the place making protests: in the Minister's office, in the waiting room of the Deputy Minister and in other sections: for example, Interior, the Press Office, the Broadcast service, and also the SS." "The Mufti was a sworn enemy of the Jews," the official concluded, "and he made no secret of the fact that he would have preferred to see them all killed." Haj Amin al-Husseini sent similar appeals to both the Romanian and Hungarian Foreign Ministers in June 1943. The Romanian government had been planning to allow some 75,000 to 80,000 Jews to immigrate to the Middle East, and Hungary (which had become a refuge for Jews escaping persecution elsewhere in Europe) was reportedly preparing to allow some 900 Jewish children and their parents to immigrate as well. Haj Amin al-Husseini repeated his insistence that the Jews should be sent to Poland, where they could be kept under "active surveillance." He knew exactly what was taking place in Poland.

In 1944, shortly before the end of the Second World War, the allied forces issued a warrant for the arrest of Haj Amin al-Husseini (again). In the first week of May 1945, as the third Reich neared unconditional surrender, al-Husseini fled the Austrian Mountain resort of Badgastein, leaving behind his personal papers, compiled since 1940. The US Army found the material, analysed and indexed it, and then archived it. They secretly shared it with the Israelis, but only released it to the public many decades later. This is partly why so few people know about such a prominent and influential figure in the treatment of the Jews during the Second World War.

Upon the end of the war, he came under French protection, and then sought refuge in Cairo, Egypt to avoid prosecution for war crimes.

In the lead-up to the 1948 Arab / Israeli war, Haj Amin al-Husseini opposed both the 1947 UN Partition Plan and King Abdullah's designs to annex the Arab part of British Mandatory Palestine to Jordan, and, failing to gain command of the "Arab rescue army" (jaysh al-inqadh al-'arabi) formed with the backing of the Arab League, built his own militia, al-jihad al-muqaddas. In September 1948, he participated in the establishment of an All-Palestine Government. Seated in Egyptian-ruled Gaza, this government won limited recognition by Arab states and was eventually dissolved by Egyptian president Gamal Abdel Nasser in 1959. However, his influence in the development of Arab hatred of Jews was huge and continued in Egypt during the 50s and 60s, as al-Husseini personally mentored his nephew, Yaser Arafat, the Leader of the Palestine Liberation Organisation (established in 1964). He died in Beirut, Lebanon, in July 1974.

Peel Commission

Haj Amin al-Husseini's opposition to the British peaked during the 1936 - 1939 Arab revolt in Palestine, resulting in Palestine becoming almost ungovernable. In 1937, the British government established the Peel Commission (headed by Earl Peel) to establish the cause of the rebellion and find a solution to it. The conclusion was to recommend that Palestine be divided into a Jewish state (a small area on the coast), a larger Arab state (to be linked with Transjordan), and a residual British mandatory area (including an area stretching from Jerusalem to the coast); a two-state solution that offered the Arabs 80% of the disputed territory and the Jews 20%, with Jerusalem remaining under British control.

Note that the Peel Commission referred to providing land for an Arab state, not a state for an existing "Palestinian" people. Arabs in the region did not consider themselves "Palestinian" until the idea was conceived by the PLO in the 1960s.

The two-state solution was rejected out of hand by the Arabs, who resumed their violent revolt. The Jewish leaders, Chaim Weizmann and David Ben-Gurion, accepted the proposal. In fact, so willing were the Jews for a peaceful settlement that Chaim Weizman famously said they would agree to the division of the land, "even if the territory assigned to the Jews was the size of a tablecloth".

MacDonald White Paper

Nevertheless, in order to appease al-Husseini and his followers and try to prevent them from siding with the Nazis, the British government began to seriously renege on the Palestine Mandate by giving into Arab demands for immigration into Palestine to be restricted. The end result of this action was the infamous MacDonald White Paper of 1939, which would have disastrous consequences for the Jewish people. It came at a time when Jews in Europe were fleeing from the Nazis and no European country would take them. The MacDonald White Paper restricted the number of Jews allowed to migrate to Palestine to just 75,000 over the next five years. Furthermore, after that five year period, any further Jewish immigration would only be permitted with the agreement of the Arabs. Clause 14(1) of the White Paper stated:

> Jewish immigration during the next five years will be at a rate which, if economic absorptive capacity permits, will bring the Jewish population up to approximately one-third of the total population of the country.

With a two-thirds Arab majority, many of which were hostile to the Jews, the political rights of Jewish people were completely compromised by the MacDonald White Paper. The Palestine Mandate was specifically intended to create a national home for the Jewish people and foster their return to their ancient homeland, but the MacDonald White Paper completely betrayed that; and without the approval of the Council of the League of Nations and the Permanent Mandate Commission.

In addition, in violation of Article 6 of the Palestine Mandate, the British government illegally prohibited transfer and/or sale of land to any Jewish institution.

In his book, *A Place Among the Nations*, Benjamin Netanyahu described the MacDonald White Paper as Britain's "betrayal" of the Jewish people and the "betrayal of Zionism" by the West (pages 69, 89).

In May 1939, a furious debate took place in the British House of Commons over the MacDonald White Paper. One of the fiercest opponents to the paper was Winston Churchill, who said:

> After the period of five years no further immigration

will be permitted unless the Arabs of Palestine are prepared to acquiesce. Now there is the breach. There is the violation of the pledge. There is the abandonment of the Balfour Declaration. There is the end of the vision, of the hope, of the dream.

The MacDonald White Paper was an abrogation of the British government's legal commitment to the Jews and the Jewish state.

Barely three months after Parliament approved the MacDonald White Paper, Britain was at war with Germany. A year after the White Paper, Churchill became Prime Minister in May 1940 and his focus turned to defeating the Germans.

Had the British government honoured the Palestine Mandate, countless Jews could and would have found safety in their ancient homeland, instead of being rounded up by the Nazis and sent to the death camps, or detention camps by the British; Jews who were wrongly branded as illegal immigrants under the MacDonald White Paper. The Palestine Mandate was legally binding in international law and the Jews imprisoned in the British built detention camps were not illegal immigrants at all. By the end of World War Two, six years after the 1939 White Paper, less than half of the quota of 75,000 Jews had been admitted into Palestine and six million Jews had been

slaughtered by the Nazis.

Hopes that the post-war Labour government would annul the MacDonald White Paper were dashed in 1945 when Ernest Bevin, the Foreign Secretary, maintained the restrictions in order to avoid exacerbating tensions with Arab countries.

United Nations

In Europe, hundreds of thousands of holocaust survivors were homeless refugees, with nowhere to go. The end of the war also saw the League of Nations being replaced by the United Nations (UN). A final resolution of the assembly of the League of Nations on 17th April 1946 (after the UN had been established) stated emphatically that:

> Those who take over must continue to administer the mandates for the wellbeing and development of the peoples concerned in accordance with the obligations contained in the mandates.

Article 80 of the UN Charter (which is an international treaty) specifies that all of the rights given to any people prior to the ratification of the UN Charter are to be protected, observed and honoured. Article 80 of the UN Charter assumes the powers given to the League of Nations and that anything decided under the League of Nations, such as the San Remo Resolution and the Palestine Mandate, are **still** legally binding under the UN Charter. This fact is simply ignored by the UN and the world at large.

After the Second World War, the vast majority of those Jews who had survived the Nazi holocaust wanted to find sanctuary in their ancient homeland but the British government stopped this, contrary to the terms it had signed up to in 1922. The holocaust survivors tried every means to reach their ancestral home; thousands died trying to beat the British Naval blockade of Palestine in unseaworthy vessels. Those who did successfully beat the blockade were imprisoned in detention camps; by the very nation that had been mandated to create a national home for the Jewish people and to encourage immigration to it.

Exodus 1947

Perhaps more than any other individual event, the British blockade of the immigrant ship, Exodus 1947, carrying more than 4,500 European Jews back to Palestine (and their forced return to Germany), prompted the UN to vote in favour of the enaction of what had already been enshrined years before in the Balfour Declaration, San Remo Resolution and Palestine Mandate.

In an act of desperation in the face of British government opposition to Jews immigrating to their ancient homeland, Jewish groups endorsed the idea of Aliyah Bet (Immigration B), run by the clandestine naval force, Palyam, to circumvent the British-imposed limits and get displaced Jews safely to Palestine.

Yossi Harel was the 28 year old commander of the Exodus 1947 operation. He had already run four ships carrying a total of over 24,000 European Jews to Palestine, but the voyage of the Exodus was to become the most famous for all the wrong reasons.

It began with the purchase of a discarded American steamer, the USS President Warfield, in Baltimore, in December 1946. Built in 1928, the ship had been attacked by a German

submarine in 1942 and decommissioned in September 1945. Its buyers, the Weston Trading Company, a front for the purchase of vessels used to transport Jews to Palestine, rescued the USS President Warfield from going to the wrecker's yard.

In January 1947, the Warfield sailed for Marseille. The British were already aware of its planned use and blockaded the vessel off the Italian coast for seven weeks, but then let it go. On 10th July, 4,553 passengers, including 655 children, boarded the ship at Sète, near Marseille. Such a number clearly raised the stakes in the standoff with Britain. Most were Holocaust survivors who had already been barred from entering Palestine. In mid-July, under Harel's command, the crew unfurled the blue and white Star of David (later the flag of Israel), renamed the ship Exodus 1947, evoking the ancient Israelite flight from slavery in Egypt, and sailed out into the Mediterranean.

On its voyage through international waters, the Exodus was escorted by the British cruiser Ajax and a convoy of destroyers. Harel had planned to slip away from the unwelcome escorts as he approached the coast of Palestine, but in the end he decided to ignore the British warnings to stop and make a run for the port.

In response to this act of defiance, the British fired a warning shot into the Exodus's bow, sent a detachment of troops to board the vessel and took it by force to Haifa port, from where it was planned that the passengers would be sent back to France.

They removed the passengers, and in the ensuing battle, the British killed three Jewish passengers and wounded many more. The refugees were placed back on three ships and forced to sail back to France. There, the ships floated off the coast of France for three months, with the French refusing to let them disembark. Crucially, members of the UN special committee on Palestine were in the country at the time and witnessed first-hand the treatment of the Jews in the port of Haifa, and the Exodus affair influenced their subsequent decision to support the creation of the state of Israel.

Foreign Minister Ernest Bevin ordered the refugees to return to the displaced persons camps in Germany, where most remained until the establishment of the State of Israel in May 1948. The last of these Holocaust survivors finally arrived in Israel in 1949.

UN Resolution 181

Members of the UN Special Committee on Palestine were present at Haifa port when the Exodus arrived. What they witnessed was a catalyst that brought about the historic Resolution 181 at the UN General Assembly on 9th November 1947, which recommended the land be divided into two states; another attempt at a two-state solution.

Three important points need to be made about UN Resolution 181. Firstly, it did not give legitimacy to the state of Israel in international law, it merely confirmed what had already been made legitimate in international law by the San Remo Resolution. The state of Israel was not created by the UN. When the state of Israel was created on the 14th May 1948, it was done so on the basis of previous legal agreements that Article 80 of the UN Charter protects and preserves.

Secondly, it is often claimed that Resolution 181 gave legitimacy in international law to the Palestinian Arabs for their own state. This is not true. While it is true the UN General Assembly recommended the Mandate of Palestine to be split, that is all it was, a recommendation. The UN General Assembly does not have the authority to change the borders of countries or make rules of international law.

Thirdly, Resolution 181 recommended a split of land between Jews and Arabs; there was no reference to an existing and established Palestinian state. Why? One did not exist. The term Palestinian at the time of Resolution 181 still referred to anyone living in Palestine, be they Arab, Jew or neither. For example, in a 1970 interview on Thames Television's *This Week* programme, Golda Meir, Israel's fourth Prime Minister between 1969 and 1974 said:

> I am a Palestinian. From 1921 to 1948, I carried a Palestinian passport.

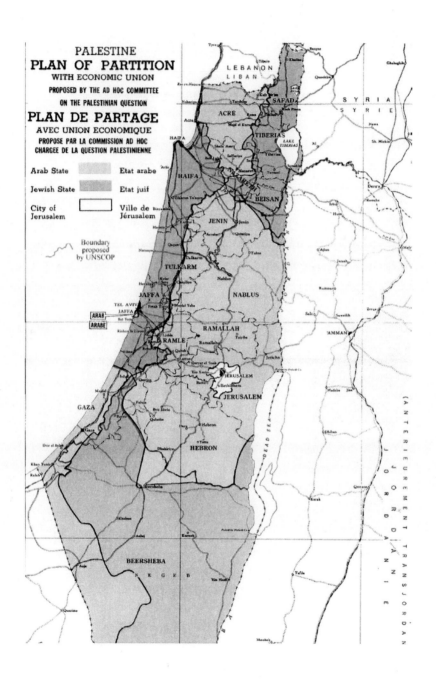

Would the **Jewish** Golda Meir have been issued a Palestinian passport by an Arab Muslim Palestinian state? Of course not. One did not exist.

The recommendation made in 1947 by the UN General Assembly to partition the Mandate for Palestine was not adopted by the British. In fact, while the Jews agreed to the recommended partition, the Arabs rejected it outright; a second Arab rejection of land for peace. The Arab rejection of Resolution 181 precludes the Arabs from any legal claim to the territory of Palestine.

The day after the Arabs rejected UN Resolution 181, they took up arms against the Palestinian Jews in an attempt to make the Resolution null and void by thwarting the emergence of any Jewish nation in their ancient homeland.

Nevertheless, the vote was passed with the required two-thirds majority (33 to 13), despite the abstention of Britain, who had by this time given notice on their intention to relinquish stewardship of the Mandate. The British were hoping the whole region would be handed over to King Abdullah of Jordan.

Following UN Resolution 181, the establishment of a Jewish state in Palestine looked certain but the surrounding Arab countries declared their intention to invade and destroy an independent Jewish state as soon as it was declared. Such an aggressive invasion is illegal under international law.

Most of the land earmarked by UN Resolution 181 for the creation of an independent Arab state became occupied territory, **not** by Israel but by Jordan and Egypt. Nearly two decades later, in 1967, the Arabs led this time by Egypt and joined by Syria and Jordan, once again sought to destroy the Jewish state of Israel. The 1967 conflict – known as the Six-Day War – ended in a stunning victory for Israel, with Jerusalem, the West Bank and Gaza coming under Israel's control.

Even before 1947 the Iraqi Prime Minister called for Jihad against the Jews in Palestine. But once the UN announced Resolution 181, almost all the surrounding Muslim countries were doing the same.

Some years earlier, in anticipation of a Jewish homeland in Palestine becoming a reality, the British government had sent Field Marshall Viscount Montgomery to Palestine to assess the Jews chance of survival in the event of an invasion by the surrounding Arab armies. Montgomery concluded that the Jewish state would last no more than three weeks. Instead of helping the Jews of Palestine defend itself, Britain imposed an arms embargo on the Jewish fighting forces while at the same time arming and training the armies of Egypt and Jordan.

End of the Mandate

On the 14th May 1948, Britain withdrew its forces from Palestine, thus ending its administration of the mandate it held over Palestine. Later that same day, David Ben-Gurion declared independence for the state of Israel and became Israel's first Prime Minister; a position he held until late 1953, when he resigned to settle in the Kibbutz of Sde Boker in southern Israel. In his famous address he declared:

> By virtue of the natural historic right of the Jewish people and of the resolution of the General Assembly of the United Nation, we hereby proclaim

the establishment of the Jewish state in Palestine to be called medinat Yisrael, the state of Israel.

And so, on 14th May 1948, the Jewish nation was reborn in the homeland from which it had been expelled nearly 19 centuries earlier. The commitment made to the Jewish people in the Balfour Declaration was finally realised. However, this happened in spite of Britain, rather than because of it. And even then, it was in only a fraction of the territory promised to the Jews at the San Remo Conference. The other mandates that came out of the San Remo Conference of 1920 successfully gave birth to four Arab nations: Iraq and Jordan under British mandates and Syria and Lebanon under the French. When it came to the Mandate for Palestine it was a different story. Following a continual policy of appeasement of Arab demands in the final years of the mandate, the British government did everything it could to obstruct the emergence of a Jewish state; a legal violation of the mandate it was obligated to honour. To its complete shame, the British government even refused to recognise Israel as a sovereign state for several months after David Ben-Gurion gave his historic speech.

CHAPTER 4

CATASTROPHE!

On the 14th May 1948 David Ben-Gurion made his now famous declaration that Israel was once again, after nearly two thousand years, an independent nation, back in their ancient homeland.

While Jews all around the world rejoiced and celebrated, the Arab world declared it to be al-Nakba, the catastrophe.

The very day after David Ben-Gurion's famous declaration of independence, five Arab armies invaded the newly formed Jewish state and attempted to annihilate it. Israel was invaded by Egypt from the south, Transjordan from the east, Syria and Lebanon from the north and Iraq and Syria from the north east. The combined population of the invading countries at the time was at least twenty million, whereas there were less than 650,000 Jews in Israel at that time.

Arab League Secretary General, Abdul Rahman Hassan Azzam vowed:

> This will be a war of extermination and a momentous massacre.

That certainly looked the most likely outcome. The Jews had little military equipment, especially arms and ammunition. During the war they used weapons foraged or specially made, such as "home-made" armoured cars and Molotov cocktails. They also had a mixture of small arms left over from the Second World War, light artillery and machine guns, some anti-tank bazookas and jeeps and "halftracks" with mounted machine guns. In contrast, the attacking Arab armies were heavily armed with the latest equipment purchased from Britain.

Against all the odds, within a year of the invasion, Israel had won a decisive victory. When I read of the miraculous events of Israel's War of Independence, I am reminded of what God said to Joshua just before they entered the land for the first time:

> You have seen all that the LORD your God has done to all these nations because of you, for the LORD your God is He who has fought for you (Joshua 23:3).

Israel's miraculous victory against all the odds resulted in an expansion of territory and the displacement of hundreds of thousands of Arabs who were living in Palestine at the time. This event eventually created not one, but **two** refugee situations, but you only ever hear about the first. Let us objectively consider both:

Displacement One - Arabs

The UN estimates that 750,000 Arabs lost their homes during the 1948 war and the widely publicised accusation is that the returning Jews were to blame for driving the Arabs out. Indeed, it is this accusation that is the foundation for the demands made that the Palestinians be allowed to return to their former villages. It is therefore important that we carefully consider the true cause of the Palestinian disbursement.

Whilst it is true that a small number of Arabs were driven out of their homes by the Israeli Army, these were Arabs who were specifically sheltering, helping, or hiding attacking Arab soldiers. The fact is that most Arabs fled in spite of Israeli promises of safety and pleas to remain; many Arabs even left before Israel declared independence and was invaded by the surrounding Arab nations.

The question is: **why** did so many Arabs leave?

The answer is because they were ordered to flee their homes by the **Arab** military commanders responsible for attacking newly-formed Israel, so the Arab forces could move freely to wipe out the Jews, expecting a swift victory, at which point the Arabs would return to their homes. It is these displaced Arabs that became known as the Palestinian refugees.

The Arab military commanders went as far as to declare that any Arab choosing to stay would be regarded as traitors to the cause. Some reading this may dismiss that as being merely the biased opinion of someone blindly pro-Israel, but it is not. It is historical **fact** that has been obscured over the years by blind pro-Arab propaganda. For example, on 22nd April 1948 – three weeks before Israel declared itself a nation – Aubrey Lippincott, American Consul-General in Haifa, Israel, stated that:

> Local mufti-dominated Arab leaders [were urging] all Arabs to leave the city [Haifa], and large numbers did so[3].

At around the same time, Haifa's British police chief, A. J.

Bridmead, reported:

> Every effort is being made by the Jews to persuade the Arab population to remain.

On 3rd May 1948 the *New York Times* reported:

> The mass evacuation, prompted partly by fear, partly by orders of Arab leaders, left the Arab quarter of Haifa a ghost city.

A report in *The Economist* on 2nd October 1948 stated:

> Of the 62,000 Arabs who formerly lived in Haifa not more than 5,000 to 6,000 remained… the most potent [factors in the Arabs leaving]… were the announcements made over the air by Higher Arab Executive urging all Arabs to leave… [and] that those Arabs who remained in Haifa and accepted Jewish protection would be regarded as renegades.

Whilst visiting Palestinian Arab refugee camps in Lebanon and Jordan, Dr. Rev. Carl Hermann Voss was directly told by **refugees** that:

> The Arab High Command ordered them out of Palestine during the 1948 war… told [them] that the Jews in Palestine would be annihilated within a few weeks and that the Arab Liberation Army did not want to worry about any fellow Arabs getting in the way of such a devastating Arab jihad. Those Palestinian refugees were bitter at their Arab compatriots who had left them homeless[4].

And it is not just westerners who acknowledged what was really going on at that time. For example, on 6th September

1954 Jordanian newspaper *Ad Diofaa* quoted a complaining Arab Palestinian refugee as saying:

> The Arab government told us: "Get out so that we can get in". So, we got out, but they did not get in.

Iraqi Prime Minister, Nuri Said (23/10/1887-15/7/1958) declared:

> We will smash the country with our guns and obliterate every place where the Jews seek shelter. The Arabs should conduct their wives and children to safe areas until the fighting has died down[5].

Syrian Prime Minister, Khaled al Azm, (1903-18/11/1965) later admitted:

> Since 1948 we have been demanding the return of the refugees... But we ourselves are the ones who encouraged them to leave[6].

Secretary of the Palestine Arab Higher Committee, Emil Ghory, was quoted in the *Beirut Daily Telegraph* on 6th September 1948 as admitting:

> The fact that there are those refugees is the direct consequence of the action of the Arab states in opposing partition and the Jewish state. The Arab states agreed upon this policy unanimously.

Displacement Two - Jews

The displacement of Jews is the lesser known one of the two, but by far the largest one nevertheless. Up until 1948, the Jews had lived in most Arab Muslim countries of the Middle East. In most cases they had been there for over a thousand years **before** Islam ever even existed. However, from 1947, hundreds of Jews in Arab lands were killed in government-organised rioting, leaving thousands more injured, and millions of dollars of Jewish property destroyed. As pointed out earlier, the seed for this violence against Jews was sown for many years leading up to this point by Grand Mufti of Jerusalem, Haj Amin al-Hussein (the uncle of Yasser Arafat).

Then in 1948, in response to Israel being recognised as a nation again, hundreds of thousands of Jews were **forcibly** removed from Iraq, Egypt, Syria, Lebanon, Tunisia, Morocco and Algeria. Their property was confiscated, which in today's terms would be worth tens of billions of dollars.

Of the 820,000 Jewish refugees created by this forced ejection, Israel absorbed 590,000. This meant that even though 820,000 Jews were forcibly removed from their homes, at no time did we see the creation of Jewish refugee camps to house these people. The Jews look after their own, which to their shame is something the Arabs do not do, and is what actually caused the Palestinian refugee situation.

The 750,000 Arab refugees who were displaced in 1948, were forced into squalid refugee camps by **fellow Arabs**, who had just gone to war (and lost) on their behalf, but were unwilling to pay the consequences. Over seven decades later, over a million of these poor people are still in these camps, despite billions of dollars of relief being paid by rich Arab states, the UN, and the EU countries. Where on earth has all this money gone, and why are they still in these refugee camps and not integrated into Arab society?

Pawns

The truth is that Palestinian Arabs have been the unwitting victims in a wider struggle orchestrated against the state of Israel by their rich Muslim Arab neighbours. They have been cynically and deliberately used as pawns in a political and religious struggle over the very existence of the state of Israel.

The Palestinians were (and still are) surrounded by oil-rich neighbours who share their race, culture and religion, but will not integrate them just as Israel did with their own refugees. For example, a homeland of Jordan would be ideal (as many were Jordanian anyway), but instead, the surrounding Arab nations have kept Palestinians in the position they are in, not even allowing them to be "ordinary" refugees, because "ordinary" refugees are eventually relocated, or integrated to a new home.

It is not as if Arab Muslim nations have not done this before. For example, the partition of the Indian subcontinent in 1947 resulted in the exchange of 18 million Hindus from Pakistan and Muslims from India; the greatest population transfer in history. More recently, Iran provided asylum for 1.4 million Iraqi refugees who had been uprooted as a result of the 1990-1991 Gulf War.

Soon after the end of the Arab / Israeli war, Jordan's king Abdullah bin al-Hussein sent his Arab forces to occupy Judea and Samaria, annex the territory to his kingdom and rename it the West Bank. Egypt took Gaza and for the next 18 years (until Israel regained both in the 1967 Six-Day War) both Jordan and Egypt denied Palestinians any civil rights. It never occurred to the rulers of Jordan or Egypt to create a state for the Palestinians. Nor did subsequent Palestinian leaders like Yasser Arafat protest this occupation by Jordan or Egypt (lest we forget that Arafat himself was Egyptian).

Why did they not create a Palestinian state when they could have done?

It was not until 1970 that the idea of creating a Palestinian state even emerged. The **real** issue is not land for the Palestinian people; the **real** issue is the very existence of Israel.

The fact is that Palestinians are treated far worse in Jordan today than they are in Israel, and many of the images you see on television of Palestinians living in poor conditions are in fact images of Palestinians living in Jordan, not Israel. They are forced to live in ghettos of poverty and denied citizenship. This is all part of an agreement between the Arab nations to **not** help the Palestinian people (their Muslim brothers and sisters) in order to embarrass Israel and exacerbate the tension between Israel and the Palestinians for purely political reasons; a fact admitted not just by pro-Israeli westerners. For example, Jordan's king Hussein admitted in 1960 that:

> Since 1948, Arab leaders have approached the Palestine problem in an irresponsible manner. They have used the Palestinian people for selfish political purposes. This is ridiculous and I could say even criminal.

This is the same king Hussein of Jordan who ten years later in 1970 was responsible for the massacre of 18,000 Palestinians when Yasser Arafat and the PLO tried to take over Jordan. Israel has never perpetrated such a crime, yet it is Israel that is constantly accused of committing "genocide" and "ethnic cleansing" against the Palestinians. It is nonsense; Palestine has a rapidly growing population.

Yasser Arafat's successor, Palestinian President, Mahmoud Abbas, admitted in writing:

> The Arab armies, who invaded the country in '48, forced the Palestinians to emigrate and leave their homeland and forced a political and ideological siege on them[7].

Those Arabs in 1948 who ignored the orders to leave their homes in anticipation of Israel being invaded by the surrounding Arab nations, have full Israeli citizenship, living at peace with their Jewish neighbours. For example, the people of Nazareth elected an Arab Member of Parliament who served in the Knesset and an Arab Muslim judge sentenced former Israeli Prime Minister, Ehud Olmert to a prison sentence for corruption and bribery.

Peaceful Emergence

Rather than Israel illegally stealing the land by force, the re-emergence of Israel as a nation represents probably the most peaceable in-migration in history. History demonstrates that conquest is the norm for the creation of nations; governments everywhere were established through invasion and nearly all states came into being at the expense of someone else. For example, German tribes, Central Asian hordes, Russian Tsars and Spanish and Portuguese conquistadors have made and remade the map down through history. America was formed by defeating Native Americans. Kings marauded in Africa, Aryans invaded India and in Japan Yamato-speakers eliminated all but tiny groups such as the Ainu. The Middle East (long before it discovered its wealth of oil) has experienced more than its fair share of invasions, including Greek, Roman, Arabian, Crusader, Seljuk, Timurid and Mongolian.

Against this historical backdrop, consider the Jews efforts to re-build a presence in the Holy Land prior to Israel's formal recognition in 1948. The Jews who settled in Israel prior to 1948 legitimately purchased land from the absent and disinterested Turkish landlords; very often paying exorbitant prices. In his memoirs, King Abdullah of Jordan wrote:

> ... The Arabs are as prodigal in selling their land as they are in useless wailing and weeping (quoted in the *Hope Simpson Report*).

The Jews did not use military (or even political) power; they legally purchased property dunam by dunam, farm by farm, house by house.

These pioneering and peaceable Jews rehabilitated what was barren and unusable land in a way that can only be described as miraculous; it was not previously inhabited by an existing Palestinian state, nation or kingdom. They made the desert bloom; they drained swamps, cleared water channels, reclaimed wasteland, forested bare hills, cleared rocks and removed salt from the soil. Only **after** the newly recognised Israel was attacked by the surrounding Arab nations in 1948 were they forced to use military means to defend their newly-founded nation.

CHAPTER 5

EXPOSING THE REAL ISSUE

If the real issue was providing land for a Palestinian state, it would have been solved and settle decades ago. However, the fact is that every opportunity to create an independent Palestinian state has been flatly rejected by the **Arabs**, not the Jews.

In addition to the proposals made under both the Peel Commission and UN Resolution 181 being rejected out of hand by the Arabs, there have been at least **three** further offers of a two-state solution accepted by Israel but rejected by the Arabs.

1967 Six-Day War

In June 1967 Israel found itself with Egyptian tanks massing on their border, a blockade of Israeli shipping and its air force – the largest in the Middle East – preparing to attack. To the north, Syria was already bombarding Israeli villages from the Golan Heights. To the east, Jordan and Iraq were facing up to them ready and waiting for the Egyptian air force to pound Israel from the skies.

Arab radio was full of vitriolic boasting about which of the Arab nations would be the first to "liberate Palestine". Nasser, the Egyptian leader declared Jihad, a holy war against the infidel Israel. Israel was outnumbered 5:1 in troops, 3:1 in tanks and nearly 3:1 in combat aircraft.

But on 5th June 1967 the Israeli's took the Arab aggressors by surprise by making a pre-emptive attack, destroying almost all the Egyptian air force without most of them even managing to take off. The Egyptian air force was so strategically central to the combined Arab forces plan for attack that once Israel had taken this out so decisively, confusion and panic reigned within the Arab forces.

Israel did not attack Jordan and begged Jordan's king not to join the war. But he did, and only because of that did Israel take control of the West Bank from Jordan; Israel would have been happy for the West Bank to remain under Jordanian control.

Historian Cecil Roth later described the Six-Day War as:

> Perhaps the most brilliant campaign in military history... the Israel army had shown itself the best fighting force in the world.

By the end of the week Israel had captured Sinai and the Gaza Strip from Egypt (which it was illegally occupying), the West Bank and the rest of Jerusalem from Jordan (which it was illegally occupying), and the Golan Heights from Syria. Israel had regained so much of its ancient land that it had increased in size by an incredible 300%.

The Jewish government was divided over what to do with the land they had gained. Half wanted to return the West

Bank to Jordan and Gaza to Egypt in exchange for peace. The other half wanted to give it to the Arabs living in the region who had started to refer to themselves as Palestinian, in the hope they would build their own independent state and live at peace with Israel. Either way, Israel was happy to relinquish its control of both the West Bank and Gaza, but Arab opposition to both suggestions meant that neither got very far, with the Arab League holding a summit in Khartoum, Sudan a few months later that resulted in its now famous "three no's" declaration:

No Peace with Israel.

No recognition of Israel.

No negotiations with Israel.

Following the Six-Day War, the UN adopted Resolution 242, which called on Arab countries to recognise Israel's right to "live in peace within secure and recognised boundaries free from threats or acts of force," as well as for Israel to withdraw from "territories occupied" in the conflict. Israel agreed but the Arabs did not, thus meaning another two-state solution offered by the Jews was rejected outright by the Arabs; The **third** Arab rejection of a two-state solution and land for peace.

2000 Camp David Summit

In July 2000, President Bill Clinton hosted at Camp David Israeli Prime Minister Ehud Barak and PLO Chairman Yasser Arafat to agree a new two-state solution. Barak offered Arafat the chance to create a Palestinian state on almost all the land Israel had captured in the 1967 Six-Day War. He offered all of Gaza, 94% of the West Bank and East Jerusalem as its capital;

while Barak proposed Israel kept 6% of the West Bank, he offered a proportional amount of Israeli land adjacent to it, so Arafat would not lose a single square inch. However, Arafat rejected the offer. In the words of Bill Clinton, "Arafat was here [at Camp David] for 14 days and said 'no' to everything".

This offer made to Arafat was far better than the terms offered to Israel in 1948 by the UN, but Arafat still turned it down and called for "a million martyrs", which prompted the Arab Palestinians to launch a bloody wave of suicide bombings in Israel on buses, in wedding halls and in pizza parlours and cafes that killed over 1,000 Israelis and maimed thousands more; the second Intifada.

In response to Arafat's decision to reject the offer made by Barak at Camp David, President Clinton told him, "You are leading your people and the region to a catastrophe".

The **fourth** Arab rejection of a two-state solution and land for peace.

France 2008

In 2008, talks were hosted in France by Nicolas Sarkozy between Israeli Prime Minister Ehud Olmert and President of the Palestinian Authority, Mahmoud Abbas. At these talks Olmert offered even more than Ehud Barak had in 2000, offering everything Barak had, plus additional land. However, Abbas walked away.

The **fifth** Arab rejection of a two-state solution and land for peace.

These **five** rejections by the **Arabs** of a two-state solution are an inconvenient truth that those who blame Israel try to ignore.

Withdrawal from Gaza

In 2005, in between the offers made to the Arabs in 2000 and 2008, Israel unilaterally withdrew from Gaza, giving the Palestinians complete control. This involved Israel forcibly removing from their homes around 8,500 Israeli settlors (some of whom had lived there for decades); Israel left homes, businesses and farms.

Israel ceded control of Gaza to the Palestinian Authority, led by Mahmoud Abbas, who was elected its president that year. They left the Palestinians a thriving greenhouse industry that exported flowers and bulbs all over the world. The Palestinians response to this gesture was to destroy the donated greenhouses and launch missiles and rockets at civilian targets in Israel.

Israel also forcibly vacated four Israeli settlements in the West Bank, Sa-Nur, Ganim, Kadim and Homesh.

In 2006, the Palestinian political entity operating in the West Bank and Gaza staged elections. Little did observers know at the time that it would be the last vote allowed by the Palestinian Authority, led then, as it is now, by President Mahmoud Abbas.

The election yielded a victory for Hamas over the previously dominant Fatah party (which controls the Palestinian Authority), many members of which were promptly rounded up by Hamas and murdered, thus eliminating the opposition.

While Hamas took control of Gaza, Fatah (through the Palestinian Authority) continues to govern in the West Bank.

Rather than use the billions of pounds they have been gifted by the west to develop Gaza into a viable Palestinian run state, Hamas has used it to build a massive network of underground tunnels and bases under Palestinian hospitals and residential areas. They have also spent billions on rockets that they fire from Palestinian homes, office buildings, schools and hospitals. Israel defends its citizens with rockets; Hamas defends its rockets with its citizens.

Apartheid?

Israel has been accused of perpetrating apartheid against the Palestinians, with direct and emotive parallels made between Israel and the dark days of the South African apartheid regime between 1948 until the early 1990s[8].

This provocative and emotionally charged narrative has been used to convince people to boycott Israeli goods as a way of protesting against the alleged apartheid. Organisations such as the BDS Movement (Boycott, Divestments and Sanctions) have been militant in their call for individuals, companies and nations to boycott Israel.

Those who make the comparison between Israel and apartheid South Africa not only expose their woeful ignorance of what apartheid is, but also betray the memory of every single person who suffered under real apartheid in South Africa.

Kenneth Meshoe is a black member of the South African parliament who said:

> As a black South African who was born under apartheid, I know what apartheid is. I've experienced it. My parents experienced it. But having been to Israel on a number of occasions, I know that nothing is happening in that country, that I have either seen or read, that can be compared to apartheid in South Africa.

Arab Citizens of Israel

Apartheid was the system of government in South Africa of racial segregation and political, social and economic discrimination enforced by a white minority against a non-white majority, resulting in the non-white majority being treated as second-class citizens. Apartheid laws in South Africa made it illegal for black citizens to marry, live in the same area or conduct business with white citizens. Black South Africans were prohibited from certain professions, educational opportunities and from participating in government.

By comparison, consider how Arab Muslims living in Israel are treated. A fifth of Israel's citizens are Arab Muslims (totalling nearly 2 million Arabs living in Israel), all of whom enjoy exactly the same rights and freedoms as Jewish citizens. They hold key positions in the nation's courts, press and government. In fact, they have their own political party representing them in the Israel's parliament, the Knesset.

The inconvenient truth is that Arab Muslims living in Israel enjoy far more freedoms and rights than any other Muslims living anywhere in the Middle East. Try to find a Jew living in Palestine who is treated as well!

South Africa's former President Willem de Klerk, who negotiated the end of apartheid in his country, said it was "unfair" to call Israel an apartheid state. If anyone should know, he certainly should. In a speech given at Haifa University de Klerk said:

> You have closed borders, but America has closed borders. They don't allow every Mexican who wants to come in to come in… You have Palestinians living in Israel with full political rights… You don't have discriminatory laws against them, I mean not letting them swim on certain beaches or anything like that. I think it's unfair to call Israel an apartheid state.

So, what about Arabs living in the Palestinian territories of Gaza and the West Bank?

Well, it is first important to remember that these Palestinian territories are not part of Israel and those living there are not Israeli citizens. Apartheid is something a government perpetrates against its own citizens, not the citizens of other states.

Arab Citizens of Gaza

Israel completely withdrew from Gaza in 2005, giving the Palestinian Arabs complete control. As part of the withdrawal, Israel forcibly removed around 8,500 Israeli settlors (some of whom had lived there for decades), who had to leave their homes, businesses and farms.

Israel ceded control of Gaza to the Palestinian Authority, led by Mahmoud Abbas, who was elected its president that year. However, since the one and only election in 2006, Gaza has been governed by Hamas, a recognised terrorist organisation.

Arab Citizens of the West Bank

Arabs living in some parts of the West Bank are currently governed by an Israeli military administration, but this is entirely due to a necessary security measure that started in 1967 after the Six-Day War, when an urgent need for self-defence arose to protect Israeli citizens from waves of Arab terrorist attack in the region.

Arab terrorism against Jews had been a reality since 1920, but until the Six-Day War of 1967, Jordan's occupation of the West Bank (during which they made no effort to create a Palestinian state) made Israeli security there impossible. After

1967, the scale and frequency of attacks continued to grow and worsen. In an attempt to end the violent Arab uprising – known and the First Intifada – the Oslo Accords (a set of agreements made from 1993 to 1995 between Israel and the PLO) gave Palestinian Arabs control over substantial parts of the West Bank under a newly formed Palestinian government, the Palestinian Authority.

Unfortunately, as with all previous (and future) agreements, the Arabs reneged on the agreement by escalating terror attacks; so much so that they were by far the worst and most deadly spate of terror attacks – known as the Second Intifada - Israel had experienced up to that point.

Faced with continuous terror attacks from the West Bank that killed over a thousand Israeli citizens between 2000 and 2005 alone, Israel decided to build a barrier wall along the West Bank border. From 2000 until 2003, Islamic terrorists carried out 73 attacks in Israel which killed 293 Israelis and wounded 1,950. In the eleven months between the erection of the first segment of the partition wall at the beginning of August 2003 and the end of June 2004, only three attacks were successful, and all three occurred in the first half of 2003. This is no wall of apartheid and anyone claiming it is does not know what apartheid is; they would feel very differently if they had lived in Israel during the Second Intifada.

In South Africa, non-white citizens were denied equal rights in their own country by their own government, but as a result of the Oslo Accords, Arab Palestinians govern themselves and vote to elect leaders of the Palestinian Authority government. Israeli laws do not even apply to the West Bank, except for certain areas with greater security risks or higher Jewish population.

As part of the 1995 Accords the West Bank was divided into three administrative zones, A, B and C. Zone A is administered by the Palestinian Authority, zone C by Israel and zone B jointly by both the Palestinian Authority and Israel. The reality is that this arrangement gives the Palestinian Authority either full autonomy or shared control of a large area of the West Bank. Israel would be delighted and relieved to hand the entire West Bank over to the Palestinian Authority if they would provide assurance there would be no further terror attacks. Sadly, that is not forthcoming.

Prior to the Intifadas commencing in 1987 (during which Yasser Arafat ordered the hacking to death of fellow Arabs accused of "collaborating with Israel") the World Health Organisation determined that in terms of everything from life expectancy to infant mortality and employment, the standard of living of West Bank Arabs improved by 320% under the Israelis and by 370% among Gazan Arabs over and above what it had been under Islamic rule.

Israel carefully controls its borders with both Gaza and the West Bank for legitimate security reasons (would you want to sit on a bus next to a suicide bomber?), but does that make them guilty of apartheid? Of course not; that's not even what apartheid is. Egypt has a closely controlled border with Gaza, which it has regularly closed for security reasons. Is Egypt is also guilty of apartheid? Those who claim Israel is guilty of apartheid are allowing themselves to be deceived by Arab propaganda and lies and have no understanding of what apartheid **really** is.

By its very nature, a boycott of Israeli goods attributes blame to only one side of the conflict, and results in a one-sided narrative being promoted that leads to Israel being demonised and ostracised. But of course, that is what the Arabs want.

On 1st April 1933, just one week after taking power in Germany, Nazi leader Adolf Hitler ordered the boycott of Jewish shops, banks and businesses. It is the same antisemitic spirit driving today's boycott of Israeli goods.

Omar Barghouti, one of the founders of the BDS Movement declared:

> We oppose a Jewish state in any part of Palestine ... Ending the occupation doesn't mean anything if it doesn't mean upending the Jewish state itself.

Barghouti does not just want Israeli goods to be boycotted, he does not recognise the right for Israel to exist; just like a certain German political party of the 1930s.

The Right to Exist

Each time Israel has agreed to or offered an independent Palestinian state and land for peace, the Palestinians have rejected it (often with violence). Surely any objective person would ask **why** such offers would consistently be rejected by the Arabs?

The answer is because **land** is not the real issue; the real issue is the very existence of Israel. For example, the Hamas covenant explicitly states:

> Israel will exist and will continue to exist until Islam will obliterate it, just as it obliterated others before it.

> Our struggle against the Jews is very great and very serious... until the enemy is vanquished.

Its charter calls for the creation of an Islamic state in Palestine, in place of Israel **and** the Palestinian territories, and the obliteration of Israel.

In its Document of General Principles and Policies, Hamas states:

> Hamas believes that no part of the land of Palestine shall be compromised or conceded... Hamas rejects any alternative to the full and complete liberation of Palestine, from the river to the sea.

When Hamas and its supporters chant, "from the river to the sea!", they are quoting official Hamas policy. When they say "liberation", what they actually mean is annihilation of the Jews; they want Israel wiped off the map from the Jordan River (on the east) to the Mediterranean Sea (on the west).

Article 31 of the Hamas charter states:

> It is the duty of the followers of other religions to stop disputing the sovereignty of Islam in this region.

It is certainly not the duty of Christians to do as Hamas claims. Islam is not sovereign, JESUS is; God manifest in the flesh (1 Timothy 3:16); manifest in **JEWISH** flesh, in the land of Israel.

The PLO's charter, the Palestinian National Charter, written in 1964, denies the right for Israel to exist as a Jewish state. It declares the establishment of Israel as "null and void" (Article 17) and calls for "the liquidation of the Zionist presence in Palestine" (Articles 15 and 22). On Israel as a Jewish state, Article 18 of the PLO charter states:

> The claims of historic and spiritual ties between Jews and Palestine are not in agreement with the facts of history or with the true basis of sound statehood. Judaism, because it is a divine religion, is not a nationality with an independent existence. Furthermore, the Jews are not a people with an independent personality because they are citizens to their states.

After signing the Oslo Accords in 1993, Yasser Arafat sent a letter stating:

> Those articles of the Palestinian Covenant which deny Israel's right to exist… are now inoperative and no longer valid.

This was a **lie**. You can **still** find the covenant unchanged on the Palestinian Authority's website. The Palestinian Authority has **never** changed its rejection of the Jewish right to the land of Israel. Arafat was putting into practice the Islamic doctrine of Taqiyya which teaches that lying is not lying if done in the defence of Islam; lying to those regarded as an enemy is permissible and seen as a legitimate strategy of military disinformation as part of Jihad (holy war for Allah). This is what Arafat was doing in his letter after signing the Oslo Accords in 1993; he was **lying.** It is something the western world has never managed to properly understand, in spite of it being a strategy employed by Muslims to deceive the non-Muslim world for centuries. For example, consider Hamid Ali, spiritual leader at the influential Al Madina Masjad Mosque in Beeston, West Yorkshire, who publicly condemned the 7/7 London bombings in 2005, but in a secretly recorded conversation with a Bangladeshi-born undercover reporter for *The Sunday Times*, said what the bombers had done was a "good" act and praised them as "children" of Muslim cleric Abdullah al-Faisal, a man who was reported in *The Sunday Times* (12/2/2006) as saying:

> The only way forward is for you, the Muslims, to kill the kufrs [non-Muslims].

In a BBC1 *Panorama* programme (21/8/2005), Dr Taj Hargey, Chairman of the Muslim Education Centre in Oxford admitted:

> We have one vocabulary in private and we have another vocabulary for the public domain and that's why you don't hear it because you're the public domain.

This merely echoes what Yasser Arafat did for years, giving one message to the western world and a completely different message to the Muslim world. The fact that he was awarded the Nobel Peace Prize in 1994 for his work on the Oslo Accords demonstrates just how poorly the west understood the deception and duality of his message.

The views expressed in the Palestinian National Charter remain today and are perfectly illustrated by a speech given on 7th March 2014 by Palestinian Authority President Mahmoud Abbas in which he said that recognising Israel as a Jewish state was "out of the question"; a decision unanimously endorsed by the Revolutionary Council of the Palestinian Authority and by the council of the Arab League. Abbas declared in his speech to delegates:

> They are pressing and saying, 'no peace without the Jewish state'. There is no way. We will not accept.

The fact that Israel is a nation again is an affront to the Islamic religion, because it proves Allah to be a liar. The Qur'an says that Allah will give Muslims victory in the Jihad over the infidels, but after no less than six Jihads, 150 million Muslims still cannot beat a Jewish nation of less than 10 million (2 million of which are Arab).

Some Muslims claim this is because America supports Israel (like Allah is unable to defeat America?), but America did not support Israel in any major way until 1973. The Jews captured land in 1948, 1956 and 1967, when the Soviets were backing the Arabs and Israel received minimal support from the West in general, let alone from America.

In his book, *When day and Night Cease*, Ramon Bennett states:

> The advent of the recreated state of Israel in 1948 created the ultimate challenge to the Islamic world… A recreated Israel proves the Bible to be true and the

teaching of the Koran to be false. Not only does a recreated Israel thrust a sword through the heart of Islamic belief, but it also adds insult to injury by being recreated in the very centre of the Islamic heartland!... The honour of Allah has been sullied (page 193).

Two Sons

Whilst the Arab hatred of Jews is today personified in Islam, the **real** hatred of the Jews by the Arabs goes much deeper and much further back than the religion of Islam, which did not exist until over five hundred years after the birth of Christ. The real reason for Arab hatred of the Jews is made clear in the Old Testament. It boils down to Abraham's impatience to see God's promises to him fulfilled, and his two sons: Isaac and Ishmael. God recognised **Isaac** as Abraham's true offspring, confirming to Isaac the promises He had made with his father, thus bringing through the line of Abraham, Isaac and Jacob, the nation of Israel:

> Sarah your wife shall bear you a son, and you shall call his name Isaac; I will establish My covenant with him for an everlasting covenant, and with his descendants after him (Genesis 17:19).

> But My covenant I will establish with Isaac… (Genesis 17:21).

Abraham's first born, Ishmael (and his descendants), has no part in the covenant God made with Abraham, and no right to the land specifically promised to Abraham and his descendants. In the same way, God also made clear that **Jacob** was the covenant child of Isaac, not his first-born Esau. Esau despised his birthright and sold it for the price of a bowl of stew. God reaffirmed to Jacob the promises He had made with his grandfather and father (see Genesis 28:13-14). In spite of Genesis 17:19 and Genesis 17:21 being very clear, Muslims claim Allah (who is **not** the God of the Bible) promised the land to Ishmael and his descendants, not Isaac; there is a large rock directly under the appropriately named Dome of the Rock (built 691 AD), where Muslims claim Abraham offered Ishmael to God, not Isaac. The Muslim festival of EID commemorates this lie, even though the Qur'an itself is very ambiguous over the identity of the son:

> And when he attained to working with him, he said: O my son! Surely I have seen in a dream that I should sacrifice you; consider then what you see. He said: O my father! Do what you are commanded; if Allah please, you will find me of the patient ones (Sura 37:102).

Muslims **assume** it is speaking of Ishmael.

But then Islam has no problem in revising Biblical history and hoping no one notices. For example, in spite of there being over 2,500 years between the life of Abraham and the creation of Islam by Mohammad in the 7th century, Sura 3:67 claims Abraham (referred to as Ibrahim) was a Muslim:

> Ibrahim was not a Jew nor a Christian but he was (an) upright (man), a Muslim, and he was not one of the polytheists.

Interestingly, although listed first among the three sons of Terah (Genesis 11:26), Abraham was not the first-born. Terah was seventy years old when his first son was born and Abraham was born 66 years later when his father was 130 years old (Genesis 11:32; 12:4). Abraham is listed in Scripture first among his father's sons because of his faithfulness and willingness to obey God, not because he was the first-born.

God identifies Himself in the Bible over thirty times as the God of Abraham, Isaac and Jacob, none of which were first-born sons. God was making a point. It was not Abraham, Ishmael and Nebaioth, or Abraham, Isaac and Esau. God's chosen line of succession and blessing was through the second sons: Isaac and Jacob. The twelve sons of Jacob (commonly referred to as the Children of Israel) grew into the nation God had promised Abraham – the Hebrews. Abram was the first man to be called a Hebrew, a name deriving from Eber, an ancestor and descendant of one of Noah's sons, Shem. Shem is from where we get the term "Semite", which historically has always been used to describe anyone of Middle-Eastern origin, and yet "antisemite" is a term used nowadays only in relation to the Jews.

But God did not forget Ishmael. Genesis tells us two important things about Ishmael. Firstly, Genesis 17:20 and 21:13-18 recounts how God promised to make Ishmael a great nation, separate to the promises made to Abraham and Isaac. Secondly, Genesis 16:12 says of Ishmael:

> He will be a wild donkey of a man; his hand will be against everyone and everyone's hand against him, and he will live in hostility toward all his brothers.

God did indeed make Ishmael's descendants, the Arabs, into a great nation. God in fact gave the descendants of Ishmael more than He gave the descendants of Abraham, Isaac and Jacob. There are only around 15 million Jews worldwide (with approximately 8 million living in Israel), whilst there are well over 150 million Arabs just in the nations surrounding Israel.

But God did not only bless the descendants of Ishmael in being more numerous than the descendants of Abraham, Isaac and Jacob, He has also blessed them with land and wealth. Yet in spite of all the land and all the wealth, the Arabs still despise their birthright and covet their brother's little strip of land that accounts for 0.5% of the land mass owned by Israel's 21 hostile Arab neighbours.

Returning to Genesis 16:12, how God's promise has come true! The Arabs would still be fighting amongst themselves if Israel did not even exist!

CHAPTER 6

MOHAMMED AND THE JEWS

In the early years of Mohammed creating his new religion of Islam, he and his followers spent ten years in Medina, now located in modern-day Saudi Arabia, where there was already a thriving Jewish population living in harmony with the Arabs. One of the first things Mohammed did was make a covenant with the Jews promising good relations. He then set out to try to win the Jews over to his new religion, as is indicated by Sura 45:16 in the Qur'an:

> We gave the book to the Israelites and bestowed on them wisdom and the prophethood. We provided them with wholesome things and exalted them above the nation.

Ishmaelite

Mohammed was an Ishmaelite, meaning he shared a common ancestor with the Jews, and he played on this in his attempt to convert them to Islam. For example, Mohammed had made Jerusalem the direction of prayer but changed it back to Mecca when he failed to convert them to Islam. Mohammed broke the covenant he had made with the Jews, justifying his actions in Sura 8:58:

> If you fear treachery from any of your allies, you may fairly retaliate by breaking off your treaty with them. God does not love the treacherous.

Persecution

As his strength and influence grew in Medina, so did his resentment at the Jews for their resistance to being converted. Thus began a period of persecutions, killings and expulsions of the Jews. In 627 AD he and his followers killed between 600 and 900 Jewish men and divided the women and children between themselves. Mohammed ordered a ditch to be dug, lined up all the male Jews in front of the ditch with their hands tied behind their backs, and **beheaded** them before pushing their decapitated bodies into the ditch. Mohammed personally chopped off the heads of two prominent Jewish leaders as part of his bloodbath, which started during daylight and ended many hours later by torchlight. Those who claim Islamic State and Boko Haram are not true Muslims need to do their homework regarding how Mohammed's actions provide them with their inspiration and justification for the atrocities they carry out. The Jewish women were distributed as sex slaves; no less than three of Mohammad's wives were Jewish girls he had captured and enslaved.

Mohammed's barbaric actions even received divine sanction from Allah:

> And He brought down those who supported them among the People of the Scripture from their fortresses and cast terror into their hearts [so that]

a party you killed, and you took captive a party. And He caused you to inherit their land and their homes and their properties and a land which you have not trodden. And ever is Allah, over all things, competent (Sura 33:26-27).

CHAPTER 7

JERUSALEM

The Hamas charter states:

> Jerusalem is the capital of Palestine. Its religious, historic and civilisational status is fundamental to the Arabs, Muslims and the world at large. Its Islamic and Christian holy places belong exclusively to the Palestinian people and to the Arab and Islamic Ummah. Not one stone of Jerusalem can be surrendered or relinquished.

(the word Ummah means the whole community of Muslims

bound together by ties of religion).

As we have already established, Islam had no presence in Israel until the 7th century.

Missing from the Qur'an

If Jerusalem is as important and holy to Islam as Hamas and Muslims claim, why is Jerusalem not mentioned **once** in the Qur'an?

Jerusalem is mentioned 669 times in the Old Testament and 146 in the New Testament; that is a total of 815 times.

Many Muslims have tried to explain this omission. One such recent so-called "scholarly" Islamic attempt is a book titled *Jerusalem in the Qur'an* by Imran Hosein. How does he explain the absence of Jerusalem in the Qur'an? Well, once you get past the pages and pages of vitriolic and baseless Israel bashing, he claims that Allah regarded Jerusalem as being **too** holy to mention in the Qur'an! By that standard, Jerusalem must be more holy than Mohammed, the Hajj, Muslim prayer and Zakat (charitable giving in accordance with Islamic law), because they all **are** mentioned in the Qur'an.

Some Muslims claim that Sura 17:1 refers to Mohammed visiting Jerusalem in a dream and from there ascended to heaven. Sura 17:1 states:

> Glory be to him who made his servant go by night from the **Sacred Temple** to the **farther Temple** whose surroundings we have blessed, that We might show him some of our Signs. He alone hears all and observes all (emphasis added).

Can you see Jerusalem mentioned in this passage? The

"Sacred Temple" is said to refer to Mecca and the "farther Temple" supposedly Jerusalem. But how could it refer to the temple at Jerusalem when there was no temple in Jerusalem at the time the Qur'an was written – Muslim or Jewish!

Some more knowledgeable Muslims acknowledge this fact and instead suggest that the "farther Temple" refers to the al-Aqsa Mosque that can still be seen in the Old City today. However, construction of this Mosque started in the reign of Umar sometime after 635 AD, three years **after** Mohammed had died!

The truth is that Jerusalem was never considered sacred by Mohammed, nor by any Muslim for thirteen centuries after his death. No Muslim ruler **ever** used Jerusalem as his political or even religious capital, even after Islam conquered the whole region. If Jerusalem is so holy to Muslims, why did the Saudi monarchy never visit the city when it was under the control of Jordan before Israel re-captured it?

The first description of Jerusalem being under Muslim rule comes from the visiting Frankish Bishop Arculf in 680 AD, who reported seeing:

> An oblong house of prayer, which they [Muslims] pieced together with upright plans and large beams over some ruined remains.

This hardly describes anything of significance or importance. The only time Jerusalem has been of any real significance to Muslims is when their ownership of it has come under attack, such as during the crusades and the Jewish regathering.

German-Jewish historian Shelomo Dov Goitein (3/4/1900-6/2/1985), famous for his research on Jewish life in the

Islamic Middle Ages, concluded that in its first six centuries of Muslim rule:

> Jerusalem mostly lived the life of an out-of-the-way provincial town, delivered to the exactions of rapacious officials and notables, often also to tribulations at the hands of seditious fellahin [peasants] and nomads... Jerusalem certainly could not boast of excellence in the sciences of Islam or any other fields (*The Encyclopaedia of Islam* 2nd Edition, Vol. 5).

Israel's Ancient Capital

The capital of Israel is Jerusalem and has been for thousands of years, as is evidenced by the hundreds of times it is mentioned in both the Old and New Testaments; it was captured from the Jebusites by king David around 1000 BC, who made it his capital. However, barely any country recognises Jerusalem as the capital of Israel. At time of writing, only America (since 2017 under President Donald Trump), Honduras, Guatemala and Kosovo have their embassies in Jerusalem. All other foreign embassies are located in Tel Aviv.

Heavy Stone

Why is the key issue Jerusalem? Because God said it would be that way:

> The burden of the word of the LORD against Israel. Thus says the LORD, who stretches out the heavens, lays the foundation of the earth, and forms the spirit of man within him: "Behold, I will make Jerusalem a cup of drunkenness to all the surrounding peoples, when they lay siege against Judah and Jerusalem. And it shall happen in that day that I will make Jerusalem a

very heavy stone for all peoples; all who would heave it away will surely be cut in pieces, though all nations of the earth are gathered against it (Zechariah 12:1-3).

Zechariah's prophecy clearly speaks of what will happen to anyone who tries to have their way with Judah (now called the West Bank) and Jerusalem; He will make it a cup of drunkenness and a heavy stone and all that try to heave it away will be cut to pieces! What happens when someone gets drunk? They lose objectivity and they stop being reasonable. Does that not accurately describe the world's attitude toward Israel? Does that not explain why the UN has condemned Israel more times than all other states combined and denies Israel a seat on the Security Council when even Syria and Zimbabwe had seats on the Council? The UN General Assembly's vote for an independent Palestinian state needs to be carefully considered in the light of Zechariah's prophecy and the consequences warned of. As Zechariah 12:3 prophesied would be the case, it is extraordinary that **all** nations of the earth **are** effectively involved in the Jerusalem question through the activities of the "Quartet", which has been engaged in trying to create some kind of settlement in the Middle East. The "Quartet" is composed of the USA, the EU, Russia and the UN. How incredible that Zechariah prophesied 2,500 years ago that **all** nations of the earth would be against Israel.

CHAPTER 8

ANCIENT / FUTURE HATRED

When nations like Egypt, Jordan, Lebanon, Turkey, Iran and Syria are in the news in relation to Israel, people's ears should prick up, because not only do they feature heavily in Israel's past, but according to the Bible they feature heavily in Israel's future and the fulfilment of End-Time prophecy. You just may not initially recognise them by their modern names. Take Psalm 83:1-8 as a good example:

> Do not keep silent, O God! Do not hold Your peace, and do not be still, O God! For behold, Your enemies make a tumult; and those who hate You have lifted up their head. They have taken crafty counsel against Your people, and consulted together against Your sheltered ones. They have said, "Come, and let us cut them off from being a nation, that the name of Israel may be remembered no more." For they have consulted together with one consent; they form a confederacy against You: The tents of Edom and the Ishmaelites; Moab and the Hagrites; Gebal, Ammon, and Amalek; Philistia with the inhabitants of Tyre;

Assyria also has joined with them; they have helped the children of Lot. Selah

Allow me to put the above passage into a modern context:

Edom

Ancient Edom extends from Jordan to Saudi Arabia (see Ezekiel 25) and is described as extending from Teman to Dedan (Arabia). Edom also of course refers to Esau, Jacob's twin brother, who married Ishmael's daughter, Mahalath, to spite his parents. The Edomites are brother people to Israel, but are not what you could describe as being brotherly, because they have nurtured an "ancient hatred" for Israel, as God describes in a personal word to them in Ezekiel chapter 35. The Muslim Arab near neighbours of Israel are not only physical descendants of Esau, but also have a spiritual affinity with Esau due to their hatred of Jacob for his birthright.

Moab, Ammon and the Children of Lot

This effectively is Jordan. Moab and Ammon, the incestuously conceived "children of Lot" are also related to Israel, because Lot was Abraham's nephew. Their descendants were the settlers of north and central Jordan and share the hatred of Israel.

Gebal

According to *Unger's Bible dictionary*, Gebal is Lebanon. Lebanon was at one time considered the only Christian country in the Middle East, with its Christian history being traced back to Jesus Himself, who delivered the daughter of a Syrophoenician woman from demon possession (Matthew 15:21-28; Mark 7:24-30). Lebanon's Christian heritage was however thoroughly dismantled by Syrian Baathists and Islamic marauders who drove the Christians out in the late 1970's to establish an Islamic majority.

Tyre

Again, in Lebanon. Thanks to the Israeli invasion in 1982, Southern Lebanon retained its Christian identity; that was until relentless political pressure forced the Jews to withdraw and Hezbollah (the Iranian backed Shiite terrorist organisation) stepped into the vacuum this left. They have consistently showered rockets into northern Israel, but that rarely gets a mention in the news nowadays.

Philistia

As we have previously established, this is Gaza, the south west corner of Israel and the site of the ancient Philistine stronghold. Today it is the stronghold of terrorist group Hamas, with a deep hatred for Israel.

Ishmaelites and Hagrites

This describes Arabs in general. Hagar was the Egyptian handmaid to Sarah, Abraham's wife, and mother to Abraham's son, Ishmael. Muslims proclaim Ishmael as the chosen son of Abraham and every year celebrate EID as a way of erroneously commemorating Abraham's so-called sacrifice of Ishmael (I dealt with this earlier). God told Abraham that Ishmael would be a "wild ass of a man, whose hand would be against everyone, and everyone against him, and who would live against his brothers" (Genesis 16:12). Could this describe any better the Islamic spirit? When Sarah expelled Hagar and Ishmael they began to nourish the "ancient hatred."

Assyria

This is modern-day Iraq, Syria and Turkey. During Assyria's height, it also included Egypt and the nation known today as Iran (the ancient nation of Persia).

Islamic State is referred to in a number of ways, including ISIL and Daesh. ISIL stands for Islamic State in Iraq and the Levant, with the Levant being the historic name given to the entire region east of the Mediterranean from Egypt, east to Iran and to Turkey; the geographical area of the ancient Assyrian empire. This includes Israel, thus illustrating the group's clear intentions over further expansion of its territory. Daesh is an acronym for the Arabic phrase "al-Dawla- al-Islamiya al-Iraq al-Sham" which simply means Islamic State of Iraq and the Levant.

Amalek

This covers Jordan, south west of the Dead Sea (see Genesis 14:7). The Amalekites waged a guerrilla terror war against Israel in Exodus 17. Amalek was a grandson of Esau (Edom). Moses declared of the Amalekites:

> Remember what Amalek did to you on the way as you were coming out of Egypt, how he met you on the way and attacked your rear ranks, all the stragglers at your rear, when you were tired and weary; and he did not fear God (Deuteronomy 25:17-18).

Does this not accurately describe the modern-day Arab Muslims actions towards Israel? The cold-blooded slaughter of the 1972 Israeli Olympic team; the exploding of buses, shops, cafes and pizza parlours; the attack on Jewish schools and Jewish children; the butchering of 1,400 Israeli civilians by Hamas terrorists in October 2023.

How remarkable that the aforementioned ancient peoples continue to be Israel's mortal enemies. These are the nations making a "tumult" (as verse 2 describes) against Israel today. They do indeed "take counsel together to cut them off from being a nation, that the name of Israel may be remembered no more." The modern-day names for the nations referred to in Psalm 83 are Jordan, Lebanon, Syria, the Gaza Strip, "Palestinians" and some from Iraq also "have helped the children of Lot."

These nations have indeed formed a very real "confederacy" (as verse 5 describes), The Organisation for Islamic States, which has pooled their influence to great effect to isolate Israel. These nations are united in their hatred for Israel as they were never before, due to their shared Muslim faith. Because the confederacy claims that which God has given to Israel, God is asked to make them "as stubble before the wind":

> O my God, make them like the whirling dust, like the chaff before the wind! As the fire burns the woods, and as the flame sets the mountains on fire (Psalm 83:13-14).

Make no mistake, a terrible destruction is coming to the Arab world, when the Psalmist says it will "set the mountains on fire." The coming destruction for their treatment of Israel will involve the obliteration of Damascus (Isaiah 17), the cities of the east side of the Jordan River (Jeremiah 49) and Egypt (Isaiah 19). God's judgement will ultimately fall on all nations (Joel 3:1-3). God told Abram that He would bless those who blessed him and curse those who cursed him (Genesis 12:3).

CHAPTER 9

CONCLUSION

The Inconvenient Truth

In conclusion, is the above picture a fair and accurate representation of Israel?

Hardly.

Those who believe it is have a number of inconvenient truths to face.

It is an inconvenient truth that Israel has free speech, free press, independent courts, open and fair elections and religious tolerance. Women have full and equal rights in Israel and are active in every profession, including the military. **None** of this can be said of any Israel's Arab Muslim neighbours.

Tel Aviv hosts one of the largest gay pride parades in the world and the only one in the Middle East.

Israel is the most free, democratic, liberal, pluralistic and tolerant nation in the whole of the Middle East.

A fifth of Israel's citizens are Arab Muslims, all of whom enjoy exactly the same rights and freedoms as Jewish citizens. They hold key positions in the nation's courts, press and government. In fact, they have their own political party representing them in the Israel's parliament, the Knesset. The inconvenient truth is that Muslims living in Israel enjoy more freedom and rights than **any** other Muslims in the Middle East.

Fighting for Survival

It is an inconvenient truth that every military action Israel has taken has been to protect itself. Israel is a defensive state, **not** an aggressor. If the Muslim Arabs put down their weapons tomorrow there would be instant peace in the Middle East, but if Israel put down its weapons it would very swiftly be annihilated and wiped off the map "from the river to the sea".

At the rebirth of the state of Israel in May 1948, it was immediately attacked and invaded by its Arab neigbours, whose goal was not to contain the tiny new state of Israel but to annihilate it. No nation came to Israel's defence; not

America, Britain, nor anyone. They all expected Israel to be wiped off the face of the earth and did nothing to prevent it. But Israel won.

20 years later in 1967, Israel's Arab neighbours again sought to annihilate it. Again, Israel prevailed; as it did again in 1973.

1948, 1967 and 1973 are the main wars but not the only acts of violence and aggression Israel has had to defend itself against. There is barely a single day that goes by without Israel suffering some act of terror and violence. There have been two bloody waves of terror called Intifadas in the late 1980s and early 2000s, when Israelis were blown up on buses, at restaurants, wedding halls and night clubs.

There have been attacks and incursions from terror groups from Hezbollah in Lebanon and Hamas in Gaza, even after Israel completely withdrew from that territory in 2005, leaving every home, community, business, farm and structure for the Gazans to use as they pleased. How did the Gazans react? They launched thousands of rockets on Israeli civilians.

In between the wars and terror attacks Israel has sought peace with its neighbours and has successfully achieved peace treaties with Egypt and Jordan. In 1978, Israel gave back Egypt the entire Sinai Peninsula - an area larger than Israel itself and with oil – in agreement for peace. For others however, every Israeli gesture of peace has been met with incitement and violence.

It is an inconvenient truth that Israel has offered the Palestinians a two-state solution and land for peace no less than **five** times, but their offer has been rejected each and every time (often accompanied with violence).

Legal Owners

It is an inconvenient truth that the Jews are not occupying a land stolen from an indigenous Arab nation of Palestinians. The land of Israel belongs to the Jews and, as has been demonstrated in previous chapters, this has been recognised in international law.

However, the greatest inconvenient truth is that the land of Israel belongs to the Jews because God has given it to them as a permanent possession. Israel belongs to the Jews because the Jews and the land belong to God (Leviticus 25:23), and God **gave** the land to the Jews. God, through His prophets, promised that the Jews would return to the land of their ancestors and would be reformed as a nation. These Divine promises were miraculously fulfilled in May 1948. Just a few examples of these prophecies are:

> That the LORD your God will bring you back from captivity, and have compassion on you, and gather you again from all the nations where the LORD your God has scattered you (Deuteronomy 30:3).
>
> For thus says the Lord GOD: 'Indeed I Myself will search for My sheep and seek them out. As a shepherd seeks out his flock on the day he is among his scattered sheep, so will I seek out My sheep and deliver them from all the places where they were scattered on a cloudy and dark day. And I will bring them out from the peoples and gather them from the countries, and will bring them to their own land; I will feed them on the mountains of Israel, in the valleys and in all the inhabited places of the country' (Ezekiel 34:11-13).
>
> For I will take you from among the nations, gather

you out of all countries, and bring you into your own land (Ezekiel 36:24).

God promised to regather His people back to their "**own land**".

> Hear the word of the LORD, O nations, and declare it in the isles afar off, and say, 'He who scattered Israel will gather him, and keep him as a shepherd does his flock' (Jeremiah 31:10).
>
> Fear not, for I am with you; I will bring your descendants from the east, and gather you from the west; I will say to the north, 'Give them up!' And to the south, 'Do not keep them back!' Bring My sons from afar, and My daughters from the ends of the earth— Everyone who is called by My name, whom I have created for My glory; I have formed him, yes, I have made him." Bring out the blind people who have eyes, and the deaf who have ears (Isaiah 43:5-8).

In Isaiah 66:7-8, the prophet foreshadowed the re-birth of Israel in one day, which was miraculously fulfilled on 14th May 1948; Israel's status as a sovereign nation **was** established and reaffirmed during the course of a single day.

In Ezekiel 37:21-22, the prophet said that God would one day bring the people of Israel back to the land as a united nation. At the time of Ezekiel giving this prophecy (between 593-571 BC) the people of Israel were already divided between two separate kingdoms (Judah and Israel), and both kingdoms had been conquered by foreign invaders who had forced many Jews (including Ezekiel) into exile. But when the Jews reclaimed sovereignty in 1948, they did so as a united people, creating **one** nation – Israel.

Deuteronomy 30:3-5 says that the Jews would be scattered worldwide, but that they would later return to their homeland and have their fortunes restored. This prophecy began to be fulfilled in modern times during the 1800s when Jews began to return to Israel from as far away as China, America, Russia and South Africa. Today, in spite of not having the oil wealth of its Arab neighbours, Israel is among the world's most prosperous countries. For example, in 1999 Israel's per capital Gross Domestic Product (GDP) was twice that of its neighbouring countries.

Jewish achievements in the world at large are nothing short of astonishing. Approximately 0.19% of the world's population is Jewish; about one person in every 520. It would therefore perhaps not be unreasonable to expect that 0.19% of the world's scientists, musicians, entertainers, writers etc to be Jewish. Not so. Just even looking at the period since the 19th Century we find that approximately **25%** of the world's scientists have been Jewish. **25%!** Not only that, approximately 22% of all Nobel Prize winners during the 20th Century were Jewish. God has prospered the Jews and prospered the world through them. But yet the world despises the Jews, because the root cause is **spiritual**.

Fruitful Land

Before Jews started to return to Israel in number, the land was (as we have already established) desolate and unproductive. But during the 1900s, when the number of Jews returning to their homeland began to increase, they built a network of irrigation systems. Furthermore, during the past century over 200 million trees have been planted, which has changed the whole eco-system and environment. This is no coincidence. In Isaiah 41:18-20, the prophet predicted this very thing would happen because **God** would do it:

> I will open rivers in desolate heights, and fountains in
> the midst of the valleys; I will make the wilderness a
> pool of water, and the dry land springs of water. I will
> plant in the wilderness the cedar and the acacia tree,
> the myrtle and the oil tree; I will set in the desert the
> cypress tree and the pine and the box tree together, that
> they may see and know, and consider and understand
> together, that the hand of the LORD has done this,
> and the Holy One of Israel has created it.

Not only this, but Isaiah also prophesied (in Isaiah 27:6)
that Israel would blossom and fill the world with its fruit.
This prophecy has at least in part been already fulfilled in
our lifetime both literally and symbolically, because Israel
is a leading producer of agricultural products, exporting
food to many countries. This prophecy has also of course
been fulfilled symbolically with the worldwide spread of
Christianity:

> Those who come He shall cause to take root in Jacob;
> Israel shall blossom and bud, and fill the face of the
> world with fruit (Isaiah 27:6).

Amos also prophesied that God would return His people
Israel to the land, never to be pulled up again, and they would
make the land fruitful and productive:

> I will bring back the captives of My people Israel; they
> shall build the waste cities and inhabit them; they shall
> plant vineyards and drink wine from them; they shall
> also make gardens and eat fruit from them. I will plant
> them in their land, and no longer shall they be pulled

up from the land I have given them," says the LORD your God (Amos 9:14-15).

In Isaiah 51:3, the prophet declared that God would restore Israel and make it a paradise, like the Garden of Eden. This foreshadows what is happening in Israel today as a result of the Jews irrigating, cultivating and reconditioning the land from the 1900s onwards. Many of the country's malaria infested swamps have been converted into productive farmland, and water from the Sea of Galilee has been channelled through portions of the deserts allowing them to bloom. This is a land that was described in the 1800s as a wasteland! But as you look at a satellite image of the Middle East today, you will easily be able to identify Israel by the fact that it is the only green area in the whole region, (*represented as the dark grey area*).

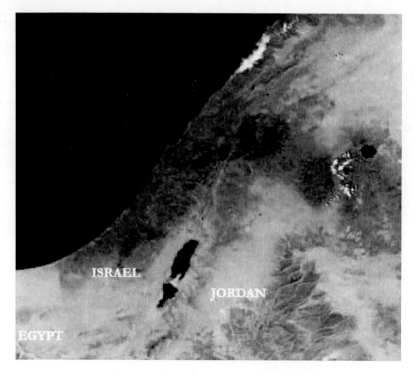

Prophecy Fulfilled

Whilst Israel was a nation during the lifetime of Jesus, He prophesied the destruction of Jerusalem and the scattering of the Jews amongst the nations, but that Israel would be a nation again:

> But when you see Jerusalem surrounded by armies, then know that its desolation is near. Then let those who are in Judea flee to the mountains, let those who are in the midst of her depart, and let not those who are in the country enter her. For these are the days of vengeance, that all things which are written may be fulfilled. But woe to those who are pregnant and to those who are nursing babies in those days! For there will be great distress in the land and wrath upon this people. And they will fall by the edge of the sword, and be led away captive into all nations. And Jerusalem will be trampled by Gentiles until the times of the Gentiles are fulfilled (Luke 21:20-24).

This prophecy by Jesus was partially fulfilled in 70 AD with the destruction of the Second Temple and the partial scattering of the Jews. Interestingly, whilst historical writers such as Josephus documented the death toll at over 1 million Jews, there is no record of any believer in Jesus being among the dead. This is because when the Jewish believers saw the Roman forces gathering in preparation for their attack on Jerusalem, they took heed of Christ's prophetic warning, took advantage of a temporary withdrawal of the Roman legions and fled Jerusalem.

How wonderfully accurate Christ's prophecy was to the point that He foreknew decades in advance that the Romans would attack Jerusalem, but circumstances beyond the control of the Romans would first dictate that they temporarily withdraw, thus giving the Jewish believers in Christ in Jerusalem opportunity to heed Christ's warning and escape unharmed.

Christ's remarkable (but often conveniently ignored) prophecy in Luke 21 was of course fulfilled further in 135 AD with the more thorough scattering of the Jews from the land of Israel, and this remained so until 1948 when Israel was miraculously reborn as a nation. No other race, civilisation or nation on earth has ever done this, because only the Jews are God's chosen people.

It is an inconvenient truth for the world that the Jews have a legal and historical right to the land called Israel. Genesis 15:18 declared to Abram:

> To your descendants I have given this land, from the river of Egypt to the great river, the River Euphrates.

God then later confirmed this promise to Abraham's son Isaac, and Isaac's son Jacob (later of course renamed Israel by God Himself).

When the Israelites were about to invade the Promised Land under God's instruction, God reiterated the land promise and this is recorded in Joshua 1:4:

> From the wilderness and this Lebanon as far as the great river, the River Euphrates, all the land of the Hittites, and to the Great Sea toward the going down of the sun, shall be your territory.

Bearing in mind the promises made by God to the Israelites in Genesis 15:18 and Joshua 1:4, the land God gave to the

Israelites included everything "from the river of Egypt to the great river, the River Euphrates" to Lebanon (north to south) and everything from the Mediterranean Sea to the Euphrates River (west to east). In modern-day terms, the land given to the Israelites from God covers all the land modern Israel currently possesses, plus all the land occupied by the Palestinians (the West Bank and Gaza), plus some of Egypt and Syria, plus all of Jordan, plus some of Saudi Arabia and Iraq. It is an inconvenient truth that Israel in fact currently possesses only a **fraction** of the land promised to them by God.

In September 2013, Israeli Prime Minister Benjamin Netanyahu declared before the UN General Assembly:

> In our time the biblical prophesies are being realised. As the prophet Amos said, they shall rebuild ruin cities and inhabit them. They shall plant vineyards and drink their wine. They shall till gardens and eat their fruit. And I will plant them upon their soil never to be uprooted again. Ladies and gentleman, the people of Israel have come home never to be uprooted again.

Netanyahu is absolutely correct; the people of Israel **have** come home **never** to be uprooted again.

How can I (or Netanyahu) be so sure of that fact?

The answer is very simple: Isaiah 11 tells us that Israel would be restored to the land for a second and **final** time (Isaiah 11:11 to be precise). The Jews have only been exiled from their land **twice**, so their restoration in 1948 was the second and **final** restoration. Isaiah made his remarkable prophecy before Israel was even exiled the first time. Verse 12 of Isaiah

11 declares that God would regather Israel the second time "from the four corners of the earth". The first time God returned Israel to the land it was from exile in Babylon. The second and final time in 1948 **was** "from the four corners of the earth."

Restoration One

The nation of Israel was torn in two after Solomon's death in around 931 BC, with the kingdoms of Judah and Israel living in bitter estrangement from each other. In 722 BC the kingdom of Israel was exiled (known to the Jews as Galut) to Assyria, with Judah capitulating to Babylon little more than a century later. This was the first time the Jews were exiled from their land. History tells us that the Jews were restored to their land 70 years later in fulfilment of the prophecy in Jeremiah chapter 25. Isaiah, who died over a century earlier, also spoke of this in Isaiah 48:12-22. The great prophet of the exile was Ezekiel and he too reminded the Jews of a return to the land, but he also spoke of **another** return, one that was far off into the future.

Restoration Two

The second time the Jews were exiled from their land, it occurred in stages, just like the first exile. It happened partially in 70 AD and then fully in 135 AD, when the Romans renamed the land Palestine (the Latin word Palaestina). In Luke chapter 21 we read how Jesus Himself prophesied the destruction of the temple and the scattering of the Jews, until the times of the Gentiles are fulfilled at the end of the age (hence the eschatological significance of Israel's second and final return to their land in 1948). The Jews remained exiled from their homeland until 1948, when they became a nation again for the **second and final time**, in fulfilment of Isaiah 11 and in fulfilment of Jesus' own words.

Restoration two; the **final** restoration.

The inconvenient truth that most of the world does not want to hear is that Israel is here to stay; they are going nowhere.

CHAPTER 10

HAS THE CHURCH
REPLACED ISRAEL?

It is an inconvenient truth for many Christians that the Jews remain God's chosen people, through which He brought His Son Jesus Christ to be the Saviour of the world. It is an inconvenient truth for those who hold to a Replacement Theology[9], which teaches the church has replaced Israel in God's plan, the Jews are no longer God's chosen people, and God does not have specific future plans for the nation of Israel. Replacement Theology has more recently been rebranded as

Replacement Theology ?

No
thank you !

Fulfilment Theology[10] by people like former Bishop of Durham, N. T. Wright, but both teach that the many promises made to Israel in the Bible are fulfilled in Christ and, by implication of the Church being the body of Christ[11], they are therefore also fulfilled in the Church (not Israel). This is **serious** error that leads to Christians sharing the world's view of Israel, rather than having a Biblical view of Israel.

It is an error that leads to Christians denying the Jews the right to the land of Israel because the prophecies in Scripture concerning the blessing and restoration of Israel to the Promised Land are "spiritualised" and "allegorised" into promises of God's blessing for the Church. The interpretation of Isaiah 11:12 given by proponents of Replacement Theology is a perfect example of this, because they say the fulfilment of the regathering of "the dispersed of Judah from the four corners of the earth" is the coming of the Gentiles from the east, west, north and south into the kingdom of God. The events of 1948 make that interpretation look very silly and empty indeed. Israel's **physical** rebirth as a nation in accordance with Biblical prophecy is an inconvenient truth to proponents of Replacement Theology who view the promises of restoration to Israel as not being literal. The events of 1948 prove them totally wrong.

Augustine

Replacement Theology is by no means a new error; it originated with Augustine of Hippo during the fourth and fifth century after the birth of Christ, who pioneered a kind of Darwinian "survival-of-the-fittest" theological system which centred on the Church as the new people of God. He believed Israel was finished with and Old Testament prophecies about Israel that remained unfulfilled during his lifetime were to be reinterpreted spiritually or allegorically and applied to the Church. In order to apply to the Church Old Testament prophesies about Israel, he taught that the Church has always existed in some form; that before Christ, the Church took the form of God's people Israel, with the Church therefore receiving from God the Abrahamic covenant, the Mosaic Law and the promises of the kingdom. You can see this erroneous doctrine of Augustine's in the teaching of modern-day proponents of Replacement Theology. For example, in his *Systematic Theology: An Introduction to Biblical Doctrine*, Professor of Theology and Biblical Studies at Phoenix Seminary, Wayne Grudem, states:

> The church is the community of all true believers for all time... both believers in the New Testament age and believers in the Old Testament age as well (page 853).

He refers to the Church as the "new Israel", the "new people of God" and "true Jews", and suggests that, "almost all of the titles used of God's people in the Old Testament are in one place or another applied to the Church in the New Testament". Not only that, he also believes that the author of the book of Hebrews views the Church as the new Israel of God in which the Old Testament promises to Israel find their fulfilment.

Augustine's theology on Israel reinterprets the Old Testament as the historical record of the Church before Christ. In Augustine's work titled *On the Psalms*, he explicitly states that the title "Israel" belonged to the Christian Church:

> For if we hold with a firm heart the grace of God which hath been given us, we are Israel, the seed of Abraham... Let therefore no Christian consider himself alien to the name Israel.

He also states in *On the Psalms*:

The Christian people then is rather Israel.

He also declared:

> And therefore we ought to take this saying, "And I
> will bring you [the Jews] into your own land... And
> ye shall dwell in the land that I gave to your fathers",
> not literally, as if they referred to Israel after the flesh,
> but spiritually, as referring to the spiritual Israel. For
> the Church, without spot or wrinkle, gathered out of
> all nations, and destined to reign forever with Christ,
> is itself the land of the blessed, the land of the Living
> (*On Christian Doctrine*).

In *Tractatus Adversus Judaeos* (Polemic Against Jews), he writes:

> If the Jews in the Isaiah passage [referring to
> Isaiah 2:5-6] understand 'the house of Jacob' to be
> equivalent to 'Israel', because both names were borne
> by the Patriarch, they only show how incapable they
> are of comprehending the true contents of the Old
> Testament. 'The house of Jacob' means the rejected
> Jews, while 'Israel' designates the Christians.

Jacob and Israel

In Augustine's above quote from *Tractatus Adversus Judaeos*, his
claim that 'The house of Jacob' refers to the rejected Jews
and 'Israel' refers to the Christians is complete nonsense. The
fact is that 'Jacob' and 'Israel' are used interchangeably in the
Old Testament to describe the **Jews** and the reason for this
goes back to the Patriarch himself. When different names are
used in the Old Testament for the same individual, it is often
done as a way of reflecting different aspects or characteristics
of the same person.

When born, Jacob was given the name Jacob by his earthly parents, which means "trickster, "supplanter", "heel grabber" (he of course grabbed Esau's heel as he was born – Genesis 25:26). After Jacob wrestled with God at Jabbok, he was renamed Israel by God, which means "strives with God". However, even after God gave Jacob the new name of Israel, the Old Testament text still calls him Jacob most of the time up until Genesis chapter 35, upon where he has another encounter with God. From that time he is most often (but not always) called Israel. Genesis switches back and forth between calling him Jacob and Israel. From Genesis 35:21 to the end of Genesis, he is called Jacob approximately 35 times and Israel 39 times.

Why is this?

In general terms, God refers to him as Jacob when He knows he is working out of his old nature as a "trickster", and God refers to him as Israel when He knows his heart is in obedience.

This is the same for New Testament believers, because we also have two names: the name we were given at birth by our earthly parents before being born again and the name given to us by our heavenly Father when we were born again. The second name is written in the Book of Life, according to the book of Revelation. When we behave like new creations, God calls us by our new names, but when we revert to the flesh, God calls us by our old names. And so it is with the Jews as a nation (the theological term for this is corporate solidarity). God uses both Jacob and Israel to describe the Jewish people, **not** to distinguish between rejected Jews and Christians.

If the Church is the "new Israel", as proponents of

Replacement Theology claim, then surely that should be obvious and clear from reading the New Testament references to Israel? However, the New Testament refers to national Israel as "Israel" even **after** the establishment of the Church; Israel is addressed as a nation in contrast to Gentiles after the Church was established at Pentecost (Acts 3:12; 4:8, 10; 5:21, 31, 35; 21:28). In fact, of the 77 times the words "Israel" or "Israelite" occur in the New Testament, nine are direct quotations from the Old Testament and are therefore very obviously intended to mean the same as it did in the Old Testament - Israel the nation. For example, Matthew 2:6 quotes from Micah 5:2 declaring:

> But you, Bethlehem, in the land of Judah, are not the least among the rulers of Judah; for out of you shall come a Ruler who will shepherd My people Israel.

There are a further 66 six cases that are not Old Testament quotes, but still clearly do not refer to the Church. For example:

> But go rather to the lost sheep of the house of Israel (Matthew 10:6).

> And so all Israel will be saved (Romans 11:26).

This leaves two uses of the term Israel to be accounted for, which are Romans 9:6-9 and Galatians 6:15-16, both of course written by the apostle Paul. In both cases Paul is restricting the use of the term "Israel" to describe those **Jews** who have accepted Jesus as Lord and Saviour. He is teaching that there is an "Israel" within ethnic Israel; believing **Jews** are the true Israel. To put it bluntly, the benediction of a letter is a very unlikely and improbable place for Paul to make such a dramatic theological declaration that believing Gentiles are now a part of Israel! The context of Galatians 6:16 is that Paul is defending the concept of salvation by grace through faith against the error of Judaizers who held that circumcision contributed to salvation. In doing this, Paul singles out Christian Jews in Galatia who correctly believed the Gospel of grace and did not follow the error of Judaizers. Therefore, Paul commends these Christian Jews and calls them the "Israel of God".

For the sake of being thorough, chapter 11 is dedicated to addressing the other key Bible passages used in support of Replacement Theology.

J C Ryle

In a sermon given in refutation of Replacement Theology, first Anglican bishop of Liverpool, J. C. Ryle (10/05/1816 – 10/06/1900) defined his understanding of the word "Israel" as being "the whole Jewish nation" and urged his listeners to:

> Cleave to the literal sense of Bible words, and beware

of parting from it, except in cases of absolute necessity. Beware of that system of allegorising and spiritualising, and accommodating, which the school of Origen first brought in, and which has found such an unfortunate degree of favour in the Church.

In a further stand against the allegorising of Scripture, Bishop Ryle declared in *Coming Events and Present Duties*:

I believe the habit to be unwarranted by anything in Scripture, and to draw after it a long train of evil consequences.

The book of Romans was penned by the apostle Paul, a Jew who was given by God a ministry to the Gentiles (Colossians 1:24-29; Romans 15:16). Romans chapter 11 is an apologetic **against** the false teaching of Replacement Theology, and is therefore worth considering in closer detail:

Romans 11

I say then, has God cast away His people? Certainly not! (Romans 11:1).

I say then, have they stumbled that they should fall? Certainly not! (Romans 11:11).

And if some of the branches were broken off, and you, being a wild olive tree, were grafted in among them, and with them became a partaker of the root and fatness of the olive tree (Romans 11:17).

Gentiles have been grafted in to partake (share) in the nourishment of the tree. The grafted branches have not replaced the natural branches. And if God has finished with the natural branches (Israel) how could the grafted branches survive? As verse 18 says:

> Do not boast against the branches. But if you do boast, remember that you do not support the root, but the root supports you.

But I hear you say, "Verse 17 speaks of the branches being broken off!" Indeed verse 19 predicts this response:

> You will say then, "Branches were broken off that I might be grafted in."

Branches were broken off, but it is a grave mistake to assume that these broken branches are Israel as a nation. The broken branches refer to those Jews who did not believe in Jesus and were replaced by Gentile believers. Verse 20 says:

> Because of unbelief they were broken off, and you stand by faith. Do not be haughty, but fear.

We are warned not to be haughty (arrogant) and the reason for that warning is explained in verses 21-22:

> For if God did not spare the natural branches, He may not spare you either. Therefore consider the goodness and severity of God: on those who fell, severity; but toward you, goodness, if you continue in His goodness. Otherwise you also will be cut off.

Bearing in mind that faith is a gift from God, if He is seemingly so willing to abandon the natural branches, the Jews, how more willing will He be to do the same for the unnatural branches.

Romans 11:23 continues:

> And they also, if they do not continue in unbelief, will

be grafted in, for God is able to graft them in again.

In spite of much of the Church being taught that God has finished with the Jews, Paul says God has **not**. He is willing and able to re-graft the Jews – the natural branches – back in to the olive tree.

> For if you were cut out of the olive tree which is wild by nature, and were grafted contrary to nature into a cultivated olive tree, how much more will these, who are natural branches, be grafted into their own olive tree? (Romans 11:24).

Paul summarises his warning to the Gentiles who have been grafted in by reminding them of their grace and favour and that the natural branches, the Jews, could be regrafted as a much better fit into the olive tree:

> For I do not desire, brethren, that you should be ignorant of this mystery, lest you should be wise in your own opinion, that blindness in part has happened to Israel until the fullness of the Gentiles has come in (Romans 11:25).

Paul declares the "mystery" (something now revealed that was previously hidden) that a period of Gentile salvation would precede the salvation and restoration of nation Israel.

Verse 26 therefore concludes, "And so all Israel will be saved".

In Verse 27 Paul then links the nation Israel's salvation with two key New Covenant texts of the Old Testament: Jeremiah 31:31-34 and Isaiah 59:20-21:

> For this is My covenant with them, When I take away their sins.

The first part of Paul's quote is from Isaiah and the second part is derived from Jeremiah.

Paul clearly regards these Old Testament passages as being applicable to the future restoration of Israel. Therefore, whilst the Church is related to the New Covenant, at its salvation Israel will be also. Christianity is already living in the New Covenant and all Israel will begin to do so at the Parousia (Second Coming of Jesus). Application of the New Covenant to the Church does not cancel a fulfilment of the covenant with national Israel (spiritual aspects of the New Covenant such as forgiveness of sins and the indwelling of the Holy Spirit are being realised in the present era, whilst it will reach a completeness when the physical blessings of the covenant are fulfilled in the future with national Israel); the New Covenant of the Old Testament speaks of both physical and spiritual blessing. If the Church has inherited the New Covenant **in place of** Israel, then both the physical and spiritual blessings of the New Covenant can be applied to the Church, but they are not; only the spiritual blessings of the New Covenant are applied to the Church in the New Testament.

Then look at verses 28-32:

> Concerning the gospel they are enemies for your sake, but concerning the election they are beloved for the sake of the fathers. For the gifts and the calling of God are irrevocable. For as you were once disobedient to God, yet have now obtained mercy through their disobedience, even so these also have now been disobedient, that through the mercy shown you they also may obtain mercy. For God has committed them all to disobedience, that He might have mercy on all.

The gifts and calling of God are **irrevocable**. Paul is talking here about the Jews and God's plans for them; He has not finished with them! i.e. the salvation of Gentiles should not be taken to mean that believing Gentiles are part of the "new Israel", or that the Davidic kingdom and restoration of Israel are fulfilled in the present age between the two comings of Christ.

Salvation and Restoration

An important point needs to be made here; an important distinction between salvation and restoration, because there are some within the Replacement Theology camp who do concede that Romans 11:26 **does** refer to Israel as a nation and not the Christian Church (Calvin was **not** one of them. He considered "Israel" in Romans 11:26 to mean the Church composed of Jews and Gentiles, in spite of all other ten references to "Israel" in Romans chapters 9-11 **clearly** referring to ethnic Israel). However, even though some within the Replacement Theology camp will acknowledge that Romans 11:26 refers to national Israel (even Augustine conceded that much), they will never acknowledge Israel will experience **restoration**.

What is the difference between salvation and restoration?

Salvation simply means all (or many, depending on whose interpretation you choose to believe) Jews will believe in Christ and be saved.

Restoration means ethnic Israel will be saved, physically restored to their land and given a unique role and mission in God's future plans for the whole world.

Salvation **and** restoration of national Israel go hand in

hand, and this is the fundamental problem for modern-day proponents of Replacement Theology that simply cannot be ignored:

> **Israel's literal and physical restoration as a nation in May 1948 begins to fulfil the prophecies that Augustine spiritualised and applied to the Church! But in spite of this proponents of Replacement Theology (or Fulfilment Theology as others call it) still blindly cling to Augustine's ancient false doctrine.**
>
> **Why?**
>
> **Because it continues to put the <u>Church</u> front and centre in God's plans.**

The New Testament **affirms** Old Testament expectations concerning Israel as a nation. Therefore, proponents of Replacement (Fulfilment) Theology find themselves in an awkward position of having to prove that explicit predictions concerning Israel's restoration do not actually mean now what they meant when they were first written.

When Will You Restore the Kingdom?

In Acts 1:6-8 Jesus' disciples ask Him, "Lord, will You at this time restore the kingdom to Israel?" Devoted follower of Augustinian Replacement Theology, John Calvin (who was in fact a Frenchman called Jean Chauvin) asserted that in Acts 1:6-8 there were "As many errors... as words" in His disciples question concerning Israel's restoration. This he believed, showed "how bad scholars they were under so good a Master", and therefore "when he [Jesus] saith, you shall receive power, he admonisheth them of their imbecility".

Calvin further claimed that Jesus was attempting to "lift up their minds" from the "common error" of the Jewish nation, which believed that the Messiah would literally "reign as a king in this world" from Jerusalem on the throne of David, with national Israel as the focal point of the whole world. Descriptions of the Messiah's kingdom on earth are revealed liberally in the Old Testament (e.g. Psalm 15:1-5, 24:1-6; Micah 4:1-5; Isaiah 11:6-9), but the duration of the kingdom was only revealed in the New Testament – 1,000 years (Revelation 20:2-7).

Nevertheless, Calvin regarded the disciples' literal interpretation as "folly". The arrogance of Calvin's statement about the disciples' "imbecility" is matched only by his ignorance, but this view has been kept well and truly alive by modern-day theologians who want to relegate Israel's significance in God's plans to being a thing of the distant past and elevate the Church in its place. For example, speaking directly of Acts 1:6, N. T. Wright claims the disciples "had not grasped the radical nature of Jesus' agenda"[12] and that "Jesus reaffirms the expectation, but alters the interpretation"[13].

One Messiah – Two Comings

The Jews of Jesus' day did not understand about the two comings of the one Messiah: first as the Suffering Servant, called Ha-mashiach Ben Yosef (the Son of Joseph) and then as the Conquering King, Ha-mashiach Ben David (the Son of David). They did not understand that He first had to come as the Suffering Servant Messiah, to be slain as their Passover Lamb. They wanted the Conquering King who was going to set up the Millennial Kingdom in accordance with their Old Testament prophecies. This is what the Jews were declaring of Jesus when He entered Jerusalem on the colt in John 12:

> ...when they heard that Jesus was coming to Jerusalem, took branches of palm trees and went out to meet Him, and cried out: "Hosanna! 'Blessed is He who comes in the name of the Lord!' The King of Israel!" (John 12:12-13).

The multitude of Jews that had gathered was declaring Jesus as their Conquering King and was expecting Him to expel the Romans from Israel and set up His Kingdom on earth (yet to be revealed to be for a thousand years). However, Acts 1:6-8 is set **after** Jesus' resurrection, when His disciples **did** understand that Jesus had fulfilled the prophecies of HaMashiach Ben Yosef, the Suffering Servant. Therefore, what the disciples were really asking Jesus in Acts 1:6-8 was, "We know you are the Son of Joseph, but **when** are you going to be the Son of David? When are you going to restore the kingdom of David?" They still did not understand that their Messiah would fulfil the role of the Son of David at a different time; one Messiah, two comings. Before Jesus' resurrection, even John the Baptist did not fully understand that Jesus must first fulfil the role of the Son of Joseph:

> And John, calling two of his disciples to him, sent them to Jesus, saying, "Are You the Coming One, or do we look for another?" (Luke 7:19).

Therefore, contrary to Calvin's arrogant and ignorant pronouncement about Jesus admonishing the "imbecility" of His disciples and correcting the "common error" of the Jewish nation, which believed the Messiah would "reign as a king in this world for a thousand years", Jesus in fact replied by telling them merely it was not for them to know the **timing** of His Second Coming and the setting up of His Millennial Kingdom on earth from Jerusalem; He did **not** correct them, because the disciples were **right** to expect a literal (thousand year) rule of Christ, just not yet.

Furthermore, when Jesus' disciples asked Him, "Lord, will You at this time restore the kingdom to Israel?", if Israel **had** been replaced by the Church as Augustine (and Calvin) believed, or if Jesus **was** altering the interpretation as N. T. Wright claims, this would have been the ideal opportunity for Jesus to reply:

> What exactly do you mean by 'Israel' fellas, because now would be a good time for me to tell you that I've changed the meaning?

But of course Jesus did no such thing because to Jesus, Israel was Israel the nation, **not** the Church. Even after the promise of the New Covenant in Jeremiah 31:31-34, God promises that only if the sun, moon and stars cease to give light will the seed of Israel cease from being a nation before Him forever (v37).

The terms "Israel" and "Israelite" occur 32 times in Luke to Acts. In each and every occurrence the terms refer to the people of Israel as a national entity. Acts 1:3 states that Jesus met with His disciples for a period of 40 days after His resurrection "speaking of the things pertaining to the kingdom of God". It is therefore unthinkable to presume that Jesus' disciples were misguided in their understanding of Jesus' use of the terms "Israel" and "Israelite" and their perceptions of the kingdom for Israel after having been instructed personally by Jesus about the kingdom for 40 days prior to them asking Him the question that Calvin sneers about.

Temporary Blindness

There is no doubt that Israel has **temporarily** been set aside from the centre of God's plans, and this is what Romans 11:7-11 means when Paul refers to their eyes being **temporarily** blinded. But God still has plans for Israel and the promises made by God to Abraham, Isaac and Jacob are unbreakable and have **not** been transferred to the Church (which is made of both Jew and Gentile). There is no doubt that Israel **is** currently under God's judgement for its rejection of Jesus as their Messiah (as Zechariah 12:1 makes clear), and will continue to be so until the times of the Gentiles is fulfilled (Luke 21:20-24). It is important to understand that God has returned the Jews to their promised land not because of their faithfulness, but because of **His**; they have returned to Israel in a current state of unbelief. God has returned them as a nation to the promised land for two reasons: **judgment and salvation, with the first leading to the second.**

The world's despising of Israel is nothing more than Satan's ultimately futile plan to thwart God's will and promises being fulfilled towards and through national Israel. It should be no surprise to Christians that Satan is desperate to drive the Jews out of Israel and Jerusalem since the return of Jesus cannot take place unless the Jews are physically present in their ancient capital. Satan experienced his greatest defeat in Jerusalem because this is where God's own Son died for the sins of the world and was resurrected, and this is where he will experience his ultimate defeat when King Jesus sets His feet back on its soil.

As proof that God has not finished with national Israel, Zechariah 12:10, one of the most remarkable prophetic passages in the Bible, tells us that Israel will finally recognise

Jesus as their Messiah:

> And I will pour on the house of David and on the inhabitants of Jerusalem the Spirit of grace and supplication; then they will look on Me whom they pierced. Yes, they will mourn for Him as one mourns for his only son, and grieve for Him as one grieves for a firstborn.

Regathered, Regenerated and Restored

Israel will be regathered, regenerated and restored (Jeremiah 33:8; Ezekiel 11:17; Romans 11:26). Israel inhabiting the land was conditional upon obedience to the Law of Moses, but ownership was eternally guaranteed on the basis of God's unilateral and unconditional covenant with Abraham. Therefore, despite periods of exile (Galut) from the land, the relationship between the Jewish people and the land was only temporarily interrupted and **never** severed permanently (nor was it spiritually transferred to the Church); the return from exile being entirely dependent on God's faithfulness to His covenant with Abraham. When God made His covenant with Abraham only God (in the form of the Shekinah Glory) passed between the pieces of the animal carcasses, meaning only **God** was bound by the covenant; the covenant was never dependent on what Abraham nor his descendants did or did not do (Genesis 15).

1 Chronicles 16:15-17 confirms the **everlasting** covenant of land that God made with Abraham, Isaac and Jacob:

> Remember His covenant forever, the word which He commanded, for a thousand generations, the covenant which He made with Abraham, and His oath to Isaac,

and confirmed it to Jacob for a statute, to Israel for an everlasting covenant.

As the psalmist declares:

> He remembers His covenant forever, the word which He commanded, for a thousand generations, the covenant which He made with Abraham, and His oath to Isaac, and confirmed it to Jacob for a statute, to Israel as an everlasting covenant, saying, "To you I will give the land of Canaan as the allotment of your inheritance," (Psalm 105:8-11; see also Luke 1:54-55, 68-73).

Paul confirms this in his letter to the Galatians when he writes:

> And this I say, that the law, which was four hundred and thirty years later, cannot annul the covenant that was confirmed before by God in Christ, that it should make the promise of no effect (Galatians 3:17).

The subject of Israel takes up most of the Bible and its history and its prophet's pronouncements are foundational to the Messiah's identity; a Messiah that was Messiah to the Jews before He was Messiah to the Gentile world. If the Bible is not 100% true in what it says about Israel, then we cannot believe what else it says about Christ and our redemption through His blood. We cannot judge the world for not realising these truths about Israel, but we can and should judge professing Christians who share the world's hatred for Israel; they are not on the Lords side of the battle!

> What then? Israel has not obtained what it seeks; but the elect have obtained it, and the rest were blinded. Just as it is written: God has given them a spirit of

stupor, eyes that they should not see and ears that they should not hear, to this very day." And David says: "Let their table become a snare and a trap, a stumbling block and a recompense to them. Let their eyes be darkened, so that they do not see, and bow down their back always." I say then, have they stumbled that they should fall? Certainly not! But through their fall, to provoke them to jealousy, salvation has come to the Gentiles (Romans 11:7-11).

And so all Israel will be saved (Romans 11:26).

Whilst it would certainly be wrong to claim that having a right doctrine about Israel will automatically mean someone has a right doctrine about everything else, it **is** certainly true that having a wrong doctrine about Israel **will** lead to wrong doctrine in other areas. Bad doctrine on a subject as central to Biblical theology as Israel will, if not repented of, lead to spiritual seduction and deception in other areas. The Church would do well to remember this, particularly as the time of the Gentiles (as described in Luke 21:24 and Romans 11:25) draws to an end and God again turns His divine attention on His ancient people.

CHAPTER 11

REPLACEMENT THEOLOGY
PROOF TEXTS?

The following is an examination of the main Bible passages used in support of Replacement/Fulfilment Theology.

Romans 2:28-29

> For he is not a Jew who is one outwardly, nor is circumcision that which is outward in the flesh; but he is a Jew who is one inwardly; and circumcision is that of the heart, in the Spirit, not in the letter; whose praise is not from men but from God.

Proponents of Replacement Theology claim that Romans 2:28-29 expands the concept of "Jew" to include believing Gentiles. However, an honest look at the context of this passage makes plain that Paul is merely saying a true Jew is the ethnic Jew who has trusted in God through faith. Ethnic Jews are the broader context of Romans 2:17 to 3:20; Paul concludes his discussion of the Gentiles in Romans 2:16. Paul argues that there are two kinds of Jew: those who meet only the outward (external) requirements (circumcision and physical descent) and those who, in addition to meeting the outward requirements, are authentic Jews inwardly, whose circumcision is not just external, but also inwardly of the heart worked "in the spirit". Paul's point in Romans 2:28-29 is therefore the same as he states in Romans 9:6: true Israelites/Jews are ethnic Jews who believe in Christ, and in Galatians 6:16, the true "Israel of God".

1 Peter 2:9-10

> But you are a chosen generation, a royal priesthood, a holy nation, His own special people, that you may proclaim the praises of Him who called you out of darkness into His marvelous light; who once were not a people but are now the people of God, who had not obtained mercy but now have obtained mercy.

This passage applies several terms to the Church that can be found in the Old Testament as references to Israel, thus allegedly supporting the view that the Church is the new Israel. Believing members of the Church are referred to in 1 Peter 2:9-10 as "a chosen generation", "a royal priesthood" and "a holy nation". These terms used by Peter to describe believing members of the Church are used in Isaiah 43:20 and Exodus 19:5-6 to describe national Israel.

When the above is read in isolation one can see why it is often regarded as the "silver bullet" of Bible verses for proponents of Replacement Theology. However, a closer consideration of this passage makes clear the context.

1 Peter is a letter (epistle). It is therefore important to consider to whom Peter is writing. 1 Peter 1:1 makes that crystal clear.

His letter was written to:

> the pilgrims of the Dispersion in Pontus, Galatia, Cappadocia, Asia, and Bithynia.

This really is a "no brainer"; even Origen and Calvin saw Peter's intended audience as **Jewish** Christians in the Diaspora (the dispersion of the Jews beyond Israel). Not only is Peter's letter written to "the pilgrims of the Dispersion in Pontus, Galatia, Cappadocia, Asia, and Bithynia", but Paul also points out that Peter was specifically the apostle to the circumcision (see Galatians 2:7-8).

Peter was writing to **Jewish** Christians, the "Israel of God"; the same group that Paul refers to in Galatians 6:16.

But even if we ignore for a moment the obvious context of the passage and assume that Peter **is** applying these terms to Gentiles, that still would not automatically mean Peter is declaring Gentile Christians to now be part of Israel.

There are occasions in Scripture when "Israel" imagery is applied to non-Israelites without those non-Israelites becoming Israel. Isaiah 19:24-25 is a good example, because it predicts that Egypt will someday be called by God "My people", but the context makes clear that is distinct from Israel since Egypt is mentioned alongside "Israel My inheritance".

So, if even if Peter **is** using Israel imagery to address Gentile readers (which 1 Peter 1:1 makes clear he is **not**), there is still absolutely no reference to them **being** Israel; nowhere in 1 Peter are the readers addressed as a **new** Israel, or a **new** people of God, as if to displace the Jewish community. If Peter is addressing Gentile Christians, at the very most we can say he is making a typological connection between Israel and the Church, but the connection is **not** that of the Church superseding Israel.

Galatians 3:7, 29

> Therefore know that only those who are of faith are sons of Abraham... And if you are Christ's, then you are Abraham's seed, and heirs according to the promise.

In Galatians 3:7 Paul declares that those who exercise faith are "sons of Abraham", and Galatians 3:29 declares that those who belong to Christ are "Abraham's seed" and "heirs according to the promise". It is therefore argued by supporters of Replacement Theology that since Gentiles are sons and descendants of Abraham they must also be spiritual Jews. This is a very narrow and presumptuous way of interpreting these passages. Firstly, Abraham's fatherhood goes beyond being the father of ethnic Israel since he trusted God before he was recognised as a Hebrew; before he was circumcised. The New Testament recognises Abraham as father of both the people of Israel and of the Gentiles. Paul declares him to be "the father of all those who believe, though they are uncircumcised"... and "the father of us all" (Romans 4:9-12, 16).

The fact that the true seed of Abraham includes both Jews and Gentiles does not rule out a continuing distinction for Israel in the New Testament. Nor should the calling of the Gentiles as the seed of Abraham be construed as the formation of a "new spiritual Israel" that has superseded the Old Testament nation of Israel.

Not only that, the concept of "seed of Abraham" is used at

least four different ways in the New Testament. It can refer to:

1. Those who are biological descendants of Abraham.

2. The Messiah, who is the unique individual seed of Abraham.

3. The righteous remnant of Israel (Isaiah 41:8 with Romans 9:6).

4. Believing Jews and Gentiles in a spiritual sense (see Galatians 3:29).

Being spiritually related to Abraham by faith does **not** automatically make one a Jew. Not all Abraham's descendants were Jews; just consider Ishmael!

The context of a passage determines which meaning is to be understood.

Ephesians 2:11-22

> Therefore remember that you, once Gentiles in the flesh—who are called Uncircumcision by what is called the Circumcision made in the flesh by hands— that at that time you were without Christ, being aliens from the commonwealth of Israel and strangers from the covenants of promise, having no hope and without God in the world. But now in Christ Jesus you who once were far off have been brought near by the blood of Christ. For He Himself is our peace, who has made both one, and has broken down the middle wall of separation, having abolished in His flesh the enmity, that is, the law of commandments contained in ordinances, so as to create in Himself

one new man from the two, thus making peace, and that He might reconcile them both to God in one body through the cross, thereby putting to death the enmity. And He came and preached peace to you who were afar off and to those who were near. For through Him we both have access by one Spirit to the Father. Now, therefore, you are no longer strangers and foreigners, but fellow citizens with the saints and members of the household of God, having been built on the foundation of the apostles and prophets, Jesus Christ Himself being the chief cornerstone, in whom the whole building, being fitted together, grows into a holy temple in the Lord, in whom you also are being built together for a dwelling place of God in the Spirit.

It has been argued that since the former condition of Gentiles was that of being "aliens from the commonwealth of Israel", but now believing Gentiles are "brought near", the bringing them near must mean Gentiles now become Israel or Israelites. However, being near something does not mean assumption of its identity! If Paul wanted to communicate that believing Gentiles were now part of Israel he could have said that, but he did **not**; it is important to acknowledge what Paul in fact does and does not say. He declares that God has made both believing Jews and Gentiles "one" (Ephesians 2:14) and "one new man" (Ephesians 2:15), but he carefully avoids the title "Israel".

He does not say that Gentiles are incorporated into the old "commonwealth" of Israel, or into the new "commonwealth" of Israel, or even into a new spiritual Israel. He does say that both Jews and Gentiles are created into "one new man". Nor does Paul suggest in any way that the Church has replaced Israel.

The "one new man" spoken of by Paul is entirely a New Testament organism. It is a soteriological community built on the foundation of the New Testament apostles and prophets and Jesus the cornerstone (Ephesians 2:19-20). Israel however, is not a New Testament entity. It is deeply rooted in the Old Testament with its history going back to Abraham and the promise of the Abrahamic covenant in Genesis 12.

Hebrews 8:8-13

> Because finding fault with them, He says: "Behold, the days are coming, says the Lord, when I will make a new covenant with the house of Israel and with the house of Judah— not according to the covenant that I made with their fathers in the day when I took them by the hand to lead them out of the land of Egypt; because they did not continue in My covenant, and I disregarded them, says the Lord. For this is the covenant that I will make with the house of Israel after those days, says the Lord: I will put My laws in their mind and write them on their hearts; and I will be their God, and they shall be My people. None of them shall teach his neighbour, and none his brother, saying, 'Know the Lord,' for all shall know Me, from the least of them to the greatest of them. For I will be merciful to their unrighteousness, and their sins and their lawless deeds I will remember no more." In that He says, "A new covenant," He has made the first obsolete. Now what is becoming obsolete and growing old is ready to vanish away.

Proponents of Replacement Theology claim that the application of the New Covenant to the Church in Hebrews 8:8-13 demonstrates that the Church has superseded Israel.

The argument put forward is that if the New Covenant was originally made with Israel, and if the New Covenant is now said to be fulfilled with the Church, then the Church must be the new Israel and national Israel is no longer related to the New Covenant.

Whilst the Church is clearly participating in the New Covenant, the New Testament itself links the future salvation of Israel with the New Covenant as well. In Romans 11:26 Paul emphatically declares, "All Israel will be saved", then in Verse 27 he links the nation Israel's salvation with two key New Covenant texts of the Old Testament: Jeremiah 31:31-34 and Isaiah 59:20-21:

> For this is My covenant with them, When I take away their sins.

The first part of Pauls quote is from Isaiah and the second part is derived from Jeremiah. Christianity is already living in the New Covenant and Israel will begin to do so at the parousia (Second Coming of Christ). Paul makes clear that application of the New Covenant to the Church does not cancel a fulfilment of the covenant with national Israel.

Matthew 21:43

> Therefore I say to you, the kingdom of God will be taken from you and given to a nation bearing the fruits of it.

Proponents of Replacement Theology claim that Jesus was making two important points in Matthew 21:43:

1. The nation of Israel had been **permanently** rejected as the people of God.

2. The "nation" to whom the kingdom would be given is the Church.

First of all, let us consider the identity of the "you" from whom "the kingdom of God" would be taken according to Jesus. Jesus is speaking to the Jewish **leaders** (the chief priests and Pharisees), not the nation as a whole; Jesus' growing antipathy towards the Jewish leadership never spilled over to include rejection of the crowds of ordinary Jewish people.

In Matthew 21:43, Jesus' target audience was specifically the Jewish leaders and not the people. In fact, we read in the Matthew 21:45 that the Jewish leaders understood that Jesus was referring to them:

> Now when the chief priests and Pharisees heard His parables, they perceived that He was speaking of them.

Another problem with Matthew 21:43 being about God's **permanent** rejection of national Israel is that other sections of Matthew's Gospel also affirms a future for Israel. For example, Matthew 19:28 and Luke 22:29-30 indicate that Jesus is looking forward to a restoration of Israel; in both passages Jesus speaks of the twelve tribes of Israel being in existence during His Millennial rule on earth.

This brings us to the important issue of what exactly Jesus meant by "the kingdom of God" in the context of Matthew 21:43, because Jesus was referring to His Messianic rule on earth, commonly referred to as Jesus' Millennial Kingdom.

The Jews of Jesus' day had **no other** understanding of what "the kingdom of God" meant, so they knew that Jesus was affirming the Jewish Old Testament prophecies of a literal worldwide kingdom in which the Messiah would rule from Jerusalem (there are in fact over 1800 references in the Old Testament to a literal Messianic kingdom on earth). An example of this is when the **Jewish** criminal on the cross next to Jesus asked Him:

> Lord, remember me when You come into Your kingdom (Luke 23:42).

Contrary to how Gentile Christians tend to interpret the criminal's request through their Greek lenses, the criminal did **not** mean, "Lord, remember me when You get to heaven", but rather the criminal was declaring that he believed Jesus to be the Jewish Messiah and would therefore fulfil all the Old Testament prophecies about the Jewish Messiah ruling a kingdom on earth; it is an earthly kingdom the Old Testament refers to in these prophecies and the **only** kind of kingdom Jews understood. This is further demonstrated in the same chapter of Luke when Joseph of Arimathea, who is described as a good and just man, was "waiting for the kingdom of God". This does not describe him waiting to go to heaven; that would mean him waiting to die! Joseph of Arimathea was waiting for the Jewish Messiah to commence His literal kingdom on earth.

But the problem for many Christians today is that they interpret passages like Matthew 21:43 through the Greek lenses passed down by people like Origen who did not believe in a literal Kingdom of God on earth, and used his Greek lenses to allegorise the Biblical passages that speak of a literal rule of Jesus on earth; the words of Jesus can only be understood correctly today when Christians grasp basic concepts such as to whom Jesus was speaking and the cultural and spiritual background of the time.

Bearing in mind the correct understanding of what Jesus meant by "the kingdom of God", let us now consider the identity of the "nation" to whom God will give "the kingdom of God". Is the "nation" the Church, as proponents of Replacement Theology claim? **No**. Not only does the context of Matthew 21 make it impossible to reasonably assume the "nation" referred to is the Church, but also the Greek word used for "nation" cannot be translated to mean "church". The Greek word used is ethnos, meaning "a people" or "a nation" in the singular (indeed a number of Bible versions translate it as "a people" instead of "a nation"). www.thefreedictionary. com defines ethnos as a:

> People of the same race or nationality who share a distinctive culture.

Whilst the plural use of ethnos can mean the non-Jewish world (i.e. Gentiles), Jesus uses the singular and speaks of "a people" to whom "the kingdom of God" will be given in the future; a people of the same race or nationality who share the same culture; the Gentile world do not share the same race, nationality or culture.

Furthermore, the Greek word for "church" is completely different; it is ekklesia and is not used in Matthew 21:43. Jesus was telling the Jewish leaders of His day that they had blown it because of their rejection of Him and the result of that was that He would not commence His kingdom on earth at that time, but would instead give that privilege to a future generation of Jews (who will have endured and survived the Great Tribulation, or "Jacob's Trouble" as it is referred to in Jeremiah 30:7); this generation will be the "all Israel" who "will be saved" according to Romans 11:26, and the Israel who will "look on me whom they pierced" of Zechariah 12:10. The word ekklesia is not used because the Church (ekklesia) will have already been raptured and will not go through the Great Tribulation.

The only way to use Matthew 21:43 in support of the notion that God has permanently replaced Israel with the Church is to completely remove what Jesus said from its historical and cultural context **and** perform some very dishonest theological jiggery-pokery to make ethnos mean ekklesia.

END NOTES

[1] Jerusalem Easter Message (10/4/2001) by Naim Ateek, founder of Palestinian Ecumenical Liberation Theology Center in Jerusalem (more popularly known as SABEEL, Arabic for "way").

Mustafa Barghouti of the Palestinian Authority claimed in December 2009 that, "Our Lord Jesus was the first Palestinian to be tortured in this land."

Religious leader of the Palestinian Authority, Muhammad Hussain claimed on 12 May 2009 that Jesus and Mary were "Palestinians par excellence".

On 24th December 2010, Israeli research institute, Palestinian Media Watch, which monitors messages being delivered to the Arab Palestinian population by its leaders, posted the following headline on its website:

"Jesus was a Palestinian – 'no one denies that', says PA TV".

[2] Quoted in A. L. Tibawi, *British Interests in Palestine 1800-1901: A Study of Religious and Educational Enterprise* (page 183).

[3] Foreign Relations of the U.S. 1948, Vol. V (GPO, 1976) page 838.

[4] David A. Rausch, *The Middle East Maze* (Chicago: Moody Press, 1991), pages 75-76.

[5] Myron Kaufman, *The Coming Destruction of Israel* (The American Library Inc., 1970), pages 26-27.

[6] Khaled Al-Azm, Memoirs [Arabic], 3 Volumes (Al-Dar al Muttahida lil-Nashr, 1972), vol. 1, pages 386-387, cited in Joan Peters, *From Time Immemorial*, page 16.

[7] PLO journal *Palestine a-Thaura*, March 1976.

[8] Apartheid is an Afrikaans word meaning "separation." It is the name given to the particular racial-social ideology developed in South Africa during the twentieth century.

At its core, apartheid was all about racial segregation. It led to the political and economic discrimination which separated Black (or Bantu), Coloured (mixed race), Indian, and White South Africans.

Racial segregation in South Africa began after the Boer War and really came into being in the early 1900s. When the Union of South Africa was formed in 1910 under British control, the Europeans in South Africa shaped the political structure of the new nation. Acts of discrimination were implemented from the very beginning.

It was not until the elections of 1948 that the word apartheid became common in South African politics. Through all of this, the White minority put various restrictions on the Black majority. Eventually, the segregation affected Coloured and Indian citizens as well.

Apartheid laws forced the different racial groups to live separately and develop separately, and grossly unequally too. It tried to stop all inter-marriage and social integration between racial groups. During apartheid, to have a friendship with someone of a different race generally brought suspicion upon you, or worse.

Apartheid eventually came to an end in 1994 with the election of Nelson Mandela,

[9] The term used to describe Replacement Theology in theological circles is Supersessionism. The word derives from two Latin words: super, meaning "on" or "upon" and sedere, meaning "to sit", as when one person sits on the chair of another, displacing the latter. Whilst there are variations within Supersessionism (e.g. punitive, economic, structural, strong and soft Supersessionism), all its versions are based on two core beliefs. Firstly, national Israel has somehow completed or forfeited its status as the people of God and will never again possess a unique role or function apart from the Church. Secondly, the Church is now the true Israel that has permanently replaced or superseded national Israel as the people of God. In summary, Supersessionism, in the context of Israel and the Church, is the view that the New Testament Church is the new Israel that has forever superseded national Israel as the people of God, with the result being that the Church has become the sole inheritor of God's covenant blessings originally promised to national Israel in the Old Testament. Replacement Theology and Supersessionism mean the same thing theologically.

[10] Theological heavyweight N. T. Wright is one of the most popular proponents of Fulfilment Theology and in his book, *The New Testament and the People of God*, he writes:

Israel's purpose had come to its head in Jesus' work.

And as a result:

> Those who now belonged to Jesus' people… claimed to be the continuation of Israel in a new situation (page 457).

Wright also argues in Jesus and the Victory of God that:

> Jesus intended those who responded to him to see themselves as the true, restored Israel (page 316).

As intellectual as N. T. Wright clearly is, his claims are simply utter rubbish and exposes a fundamental misunderstanding of God's purpose for Israel. It is **not** God's intention for everyone who believes in His Son to become part of "Israel". Through Abraham, the nation Israel was created as a vehicle to bring blessings "to all the families of the earth" (Genesis 12:2-3), but it has **never** been God's intention to make everyone who believes, "Israel". Israel, through the ultimate Israelite, Jesus Christ, is the means by which "all the families of the earth" will be blessed, but Israel is not an end in itself. The premise of N. T. Wright's statements about Israel is wrong, because he completely misses God's intended purpose for Israel.

Another modern-day outspoken proponent of Fulfilment Theology is Dr Gary Burge, Professor of New Testament Studies at prestigious Wheaton College, Illinois (and evangelical ordained Presbyterian Minister). Burge asserts that the land of Israel is no longer important to God's redemptive plan for humanity, and the kingdom of God, which was established by Jesus, **fulfils** all the promises God made to Abraham and the people of Israel. Therefore, there is no need for a literal "kingdom" for the Jews.

At the 2010 Christ at the Checkpoint Conference (held at the Bethlehem Bible College), Burge announced to the attendees:

> It is not that the covenant of Abraham has been **replaced**; nor that it has been **superseded**; it has been **fulfilled** (emphasis added).

Burge was trying here to draw a distinction between Replacement Theology (supersessionism) and Fulfilment Theology. **There is no difference** in their attitude towards Israel, and Burge's real attitude and heart towards Israel is demonstrated by the amount of time and energy he commits to writing **against** Israel, and the fact that he played a direct role in his church divesting (i.e. selling its interest) in three companies that do business with Israel.

Contrary to the claims of N. T. Wright and Gary Burge, the eternal covenants and promises of physical land to Abraham and his descendants are literal, not spiritual. Ownership of the land has always been unconditional. Occupation of the land was dependant on Israel's obedience. Furthermore, Romans chapters 9 to 11 confirms that God **still** has plans for the Jews. N. T. Wright and Gary Burge are right to say Jesus is the fulfilment of the Old Testament, but it is wrong to go beyond that and therefore conclude that details of Old Testament prophecies have somehow been absorbed into Christ in some mystical kind of way that makes the specifics of these prophecies no longer relevant.

In reality, the New Testament **affirms** Old Testament expectations concerning Israel as a nation. Therefore, proponents of Replacement/Fulfilment Theology find themselves in an awkward position of having to prove that explicit predictions concerning Israel's restoration do not actually mean now what they meant when they were first written. This is (to use a cricketing parlance) a very "sticky wicket"!

Speaking of his fellow Jews, Paul declared:

> ...to whom pertain the adoption, the glory, the covenants, the giving of the law, the service of God, and the promises (Romans 9:4).

Paul is not speaking of the Church! He is saying the adoption, the glory, the covenants, the giving of the law, the service of God, and the promises, are still the possession of national Israel; even with the Church in existence, and even during a time in which Israel's disobedience is evident; they still belong to Israel in unbelief. If the Church is now the true Israel and national Israel is no longer related to the Old Testament covenant and promises, why does Paul state that the covenants and promises still belong to Israel?

We see a similar affirmation in Acts 3:11-26. In Peter's second sermon to the "men of Israel", he reminds them that:

> You are sons of the prophets, and of the covenant which God made with our fathers, saying to Abraham, 'And in your seed all the families of the earth shall be blessed (verse 25).

Even in a state of unbelief Israel is still related to the Abrahamic covenant.

[11] This theology is based on several passages in the Bible, including Romans 12:5, 1 Corinthians 12:12-27, Ephesians 3:6 and 5:23, Colossians 1:18 and Colossians 1:24. Jesus Christ is seen as the "head" of the body, which is the Church, while the

"members" of the body are seen as members of the Church.

[12] N. T. Wright - *Jesus and the Victory of God*, page 463.

[13] N. T. Wright - *The New Testament and the People of God*, page 374.

APPENDIX 1

BIBLICAL HISTORY CONFIRMED BY NON-BIBLICAL SOURCES

As part of the lies and propaganda claiming there was an historic indigenous Arab Palestinian nation, the veracity of Israel's history and the Jew's ancient connection with the land is regularly denied; it is claimed that the Old Testament record of the nation of Israel is nothing more than a work of fiction, when in reality it is fiction to claim there was an historic indigenous Arab Palestinian nation; there is no evidence of any Palestinian kingdom or ruler found anywhere in the historical record.

In stark contrast, the history of Israel is recorded in ancient non-Biblical historical records. For example, the following is a list of kings of Israel and Judah recorded in non-Biblical historical sources that confirm the Biblical record.

Omri

King Omri was the sixth king of the northern kingdom of Israel. Despite his precarious ascension to the throne, Omri ruled for twelve years (885 - 874 BC) before his son, King Ahab, succeeded him. As the others before him, Omri did evil in the sight of the Lord, but Omri is noted in the Bible for being the worst of the kings up to that point (1 Kings 16:25).

Omri is mentioned in the Moabite Stele (a vertical piece of stone with writing cut into it) discovered in 1868 and currently housed at the Louvre Museum in Paris. The Moabite Stele describes how Omri and the Israelites conquered the Moabites and how, following Omri's death, Misha of Moab managed to drive the Israelites out and restore independence.

Ahab

Omri was succeeded to the throne of Israel by his son, Ahab who reigned during the time of Elijah the prophet from 874 - 853 BC.

Ahab is mentioned in the Assyrian Kurkh Stele discovered in 1861 and currently housed at the British Museum in London. The Stele records that Ahab was one of the 11 kings who allied together to fight the Assyrians in the year 853 BC.

The same stele mentions Ben Hadad II (865 - 842 BC), the king of Aram, who is also mentioned in the Old Testament (sometimes an enemy and sometimes an ally of Ahab) in 1 Kings 20 and 2 Kings 6 - 8.

Jehoram

Ahab was succeeded to the throne of Israel by his son, Jehoram (852 - 841 BC). Ben Hadad II was succeeded to the throne of Aram not by a son, but by a court official called Hazael (842 - 796 BC). Hazael is mentioned by name in 1 Kings 19 and 2 Kings 8 - 13.

Hazael's name has been found inscribed on at least two

ancient artifacts. He is also considered to be the king who commissioned the Aramean Tel dan Stele discovered in 1993 and is currently held at the Israel Museum in Jerusalem. It describes how the king of Aram defeated both Jehoram the king of Israel and Ahaziah (841 BC) the king of Judah. This is important for two reasons. Firstly, the Bible also describes the exact same event. Secondly, this is the earliest external mention of a king of the House of David, i.e. a king of the southern kingdom of Judah.

Jehu

Jehu (841 - 814 BC) ruled Israel following Hazael's defeat of Jehoram. Jehu is important because not only is his name found in the archaeological record, his image is as well. On the Assyrian Black Obelisk of Shalmaneser III discovered in 1846 (currently in the British Museum in London), Jehu is pictured bowing down to Shalmaneser III. There, the Assyrians labelled him as Yehu from the House of Omri.

According to the Old Testament (2 Kings 13) king Hazael of Aram was followed by his son, Ben Hadad, who became Ben Hadad III; a fact of history confirmed by the Aramean Stele of Zakkur discovered in 1903 and currently held at the Louvre in Paris.

Jehoash

There are two kings with the name Jehoash (or Joash) in the Bible: one a king of Judah (reigned 835 - 796 BC) and the other a king of Israel (reigned 798 - 782 BC).

The name of the latter appears on the Assyrian Tel al-Rimah Stele discovered in 1967 and held in the in Iraq Museum in Baghdad.

Jeroboam II

In 1903, in the ruins of the Biblical city of Meggido, in northern Israel, an archaeologist found a seal made of jasper, engraved with the following inscription: "SHEMA SERVANT OF JEROBOAM." The seal belonged to a servant of Jeroboam II, who ruled at the time of Jonah the prophet.

Kings of Israel Menahem, Pekah and Hoshea all appear in Assyrian records as having paid tribute to Tiglath-Pilesar III, as is Rezin, the final king of Aram, who is mentioned in 2 Kings chapters 15 and 16 and Isaiah 7:1-8.

Tiglath-Pilesar is mentioned in 2 kings, referred to as Pul (short for Pilesar) but in 1 Chronicles his full name is used. The following two Assyrian kings are also mentioned in the Bible: Tiglath-Pilasar's sons, Shalmanesar V and Sargon II. They helped to destroy Samaria and bring about the end of the northern kingdom of Israel. The son of Sargon II, Sennacherib, thus turned his attention to the southern kingdom of Judah.

After Ahaziah, king of Judah, who was mentioned on the Tel dan Stele, the next two kings of Judah that appear in non-Biblical records are Jotham and Ahaz.

Jotham and Ahaz

The names of Jotham and Ahaz (the two kings of the southern kingdom of Judah) appear together on a seal discovered in 1995, which reads, "BELONGING TO AHAZ, SON OF YEHOTAM, KING OF JUDAH".

Hezekiah

According to the Old Testament, Jerusalem was able to

hold off the Assyrians during the reign of king Hezekiah, allowing the southern kingdom of Judah to survive when the northern kingdom did not. This is confirmed on the Taylor Prism discovered in 1830 and now held at Israel Museum in Jerusalem. It records the Annul of Sennacherib, which declares:

> As for Hezekiah, the Jew, he did not submit to my yoke. I laid siege to 46 of his strong cities and conquered them. Himself I made a prisoner in Jerusalem, his royal residence, like a bird in a cage.

King Hezekiah's name was also found on a seal found in Jerusalem in 2015 that includes a depiction of the sun with downward facing wings, which is believed to be Hezekiah's royal seal, because the seal says, "BELONGING TO HEZEKIAH, THE SON OF AHAZ, KING OF JUDAH".

Just a few years later another seal was found at the same site, this time reading, "BELONGING TO ISAIAH, THE NAVI". Navi is the Hebrew word for prophet, thus providing archaeological evidence for Isaiah the prophet, who lived in Judah at the same time as Hezekiah.

Manasseh

The story of King Manasseh is told in 2 Kings 21:1-18 and 2 Chronicles 32:33-33:20, and he is also mentioned briefly in Jeremiah 15:4. Manasseh was king of the southern kingdom of Judah and the son of the godly king Hezekiah.

Manasseh is mentioned in the Assyrian Prism of Esarhaddon, discovered in 1927 and held at the British Museum in London. Esarhaddon is of course also mentioned on the Prism, as well as the Old Testament.

The Bible even covers how transfer of power between Sennacherib and his son Esarhaddon took place (2 Kings 19:37). This historical fact is recorded in several contemporary sources that corroborates the Biblical account.

Other Historical Kings and Rulers

The historicity of the Old Testament can be further confirmed by the names of ancient rulers of other kingdoms it mentions that are recorded in non-Biblical sources. Here are just a few:

The final Assyrian king mentioned in the Old Testament is Ashurbanipal, which in Ezra 4:10 calls him Osnapper.

Shishak (Shoshenq I) is the first Egyptian king to be mentioned by name in the Bible (1 Kings 11:40; 14:25; 2 Chronicles 12:2-9), who ruled Egypt during the time of Rehoboam and Jeroboam.

2 Kings 17:4 mentions King So of Egypt, who was also known as Osorkon IV.

2 Kings 23:9 confirms Pharaoh Necho II killed king Josiah. Jeremiah 46:2 also references Pharaoh Necho.

We then come to arguably the most famous foreign ruler mentioned in the Bible, Nebuchadnezzar the king of Babylon, who is referenced in 2 Kings chapters 24 and 25, Jeremiah chapters 21 to 52 and Daniel chapters 1 to 5.

Multiple archaeological discoveries have confirmed the historicity of Nebuchadnezzar, such as the inscription plaque found on the Ishtar Gate found in Babylon in 1830 (and reconstructed in Berlin, Germany). Then there is the Babylonian Chronicles discovered in the 19th century and now held at the British Museum in London.

Babylonian records found also mention "JECONIAH KING OF THE JEWS", who was deported to Babylon and held prisoner there. The Babylonian record confirms the Old Testament record of Jeconiah, which lists him in the lineage of Solomon in 1 Chronicles 3:16-17. He is also listed in the genealogy of Jesus, in Joseph's family line in Matthew chapter 1.

The next Babylonian king to be mentioned in the Old Testament is Belshazzar in Daniel chapters 5 to 8. Both the Old Testament and external records confirm that it was during Belshazzar's rule that Babylon fell to the Persians.

The ruler of the Persian Empire was Cyrus, who is referenced in Ezra 1:1-2, Isaiah 45:1 and Daniel 1:21. The rule of Cyrus is confirmed in non-Biblical sources, including the Cyrus Cylinder discovered in 1879 and now displayed at the British Museum in London. It describes Cyrus' decree allowing the Jews to return to Jerusalem to rebuild the temple, which is recorded in Ezra 6:3 and 2 Chronicles 36:23.

APPENDIX 2

PROPHECIES FULFILLED
BY JESUS

The following are just a few of the many Old Testament prophecies that were made about the coming Messiah between 500 and 1,200 years before Jesus Christ fulfilled them all (and many more):

Micah 5:2-5 describes how the coming Messiah would be born in Bethlehem. Matthew 2:1-6 confirms that Jesus was of course born in Bethlehem.

Isaiah 9:7 describes how the coming Messiah would be born a king in the line of David (as does Jeremiah 23:5, 30:9). Matthew 1:1 records the genealogy of Jesus Christ the Son of David (as does Luke 1:32; Acts 13:22-23).

Isaiah 7:13-14 describes how the Messiah would be born of a virgin. Matthew 1:18-23 confirms that Jesus was born of a virgin (as does Luke 1:26-35).

Psalm 72:10-11 describes how kings shall bring the Messiah gifts and fall down before Him. Matthew 2:1-11 describes how the Magi from the east presented gifts to Jesus and bowed before Him.

Despite the prophecy being fulfilled that the Messiah would be born in Bethlehem, Hosea 11:1 describes how the Messiah would also be called out of Egypt. Matthew 2:13-15, 19-21 confirms the circumstances that meant Jesus was indeed called out of Egypt.

Psalm 69:8 describes how the coming Messiah would be rejected by his brethren. John 7:3-5 states clearly that His own brothers did not believe Jesus.

Zechariah 9:9 describes how the coming Messiah would enter Jerusalem on a donkey, a colt. Mark 11:1-10 describes how Jesus did just that.

Exodus 12:46 and Numbers 9:12 describes how the coming Messiah would be the Passover sacrifice with no bone broken. John 19:31-36 outlines how Jesus was killed without any bones being broken in fulfilment of these prophecies.

Deuteronomy 21:23 describes how anyone hung on a tree is cursed by God. Galatians 3:13 explains how Jesus redeemed us from the curse of the law by becoming a curse for us.

Psalm 22:16 and Zechariah 12:10 allude to how the coming Messiah would be pierced. Matthew 27:35 (amongst others) describes how Jesus was crucified with His hands and feet pierced.

Psalm 22:18 describes how the coming Messiah would have His coat divided and cast lots for. John 19:23-24 describes how the Roman soldiers cast lots for Jesus clothing.

Psalm 69:20-22 describes how the coming Messiah would be

given vinegar (sour wine). Matthew 27:34 describes how Jesus was offered wine mixed with gall (see also Mark 15:23; 15:36; Luke 23:36; John 19:29).

Isaiah 50:6 describes how the coming Messiah would be beaten and spat upon. Matthew 26:67 describes how Jesus was spat on and struck. Matthew 27:26-30 describes how Jesus was spat on and struck (see also Mark 14:65; 15:15-19; Luke 22:63-65; John 19:1).

APPENDIX 3

A PICTURE IS WORTH A THOUSAND LIES

The four maps below (or slight variations on them) have been used in countless videos, publications (including *The New York Times*) and presentations (including by President of the Palestinian Authority, Mahmoud Abbas) to supposedly demonstrate how Israel has progressively and illegally stolen land from an established Palestinian state.

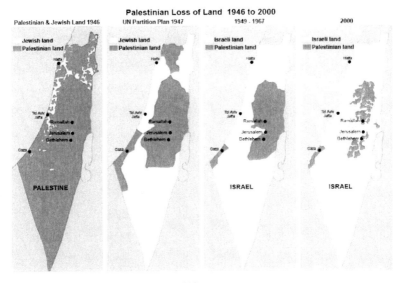

Palestinian Loss of Land 1946 to 2000

What the maps claim to represent is a complete fabrication and lie.

Map One

The white areas in map one indicates where Jews were living in small settlements in 1946, before Israel's rebirth as a nation in 1948. This land had been legally purchased by Jews many years before from absentee Turkish landlords. It was not stolen from anyone; certainly not from Arab Palestinians who did not own the land.

Because the map shows where Jews were living in Palestine in 1946, the dark areas marked as Palestine imply Arab Palestinians were physically living there, but they were not; far from it in fact. Large parts of the dark area marked as Palestine were completely uninhabitable; no one lived there.

Map one does not represent reality because there was no thriving Arab Palestinian state or nation dwelling within the dark area of the map, nor was this area legally owned by Arabs. The Arabs that were living in Palestine at the time did not even identify themselves as Palestinians, because the term was still recognised by Arabs as referring to Jews. For example, in a 1970 interview on Thames Television's *This Week* programme, Golda Meir, Israel's fourth Prime Minister between 1969 and 1974 said:

> I am a Palestinian. From 1921 to 1948, I carried a
> Palestinian passport.

It was not until Yasser Arafat's Palestinian Liberation Organisation (PLO) in the 1960s that Arabs living in Palestine really started calling themselves Palestinian.

Map one deceptively and dishonestly makes a claim of collective Arab ownership of all the dark area, which of course is central to the Palestinian narrative and propaganda of Israel stealing land, but is not based on historical reality. The Arabs did not own this land by either heritage, inheritance nor purchase. They were not even living in the vast majority of it.

Map Two

Map two simply illustrates the recommended divide of land between Jew and Arab as a two-state solution under the 1947 UN Resolution 181; a solution accepted by the Jews but rejected by the Arabs, who immediately declared war on Israel.

Map Three

Map three reflects the aftermath of the 1948 War of Independence, in which Israel lost 1% of its population (many of whom had fled to Israel to escape the Nazi Holocaust). Israel defeated the Arab invaders and expanded its borders in an attempt to prevent further illegal invasion from the surrounding Arab nations.

The first huge lie to expose on map three is what is portrayed as Palestine, because the dark areas were not under the control of Arab Palestinians. The invading Arab countries did not invade with the intention of creating a Palestinian state; their goal was to grab whatever land they could for themselves. Therefore, what is shown in map three as Palestine on the right was occupied and governed by Jordan from 1949 to 1967, including much of Jerusalem; it was Jordan that named the area the West Bank, signifying it was, as far as they were concerned, the western part of sovereign Jordanian territory. In the 18 years Jordan held the West Bank it made absolutely zero attempt to create a Palestinian state.

By the same token, the smaller dark green area on the left of map three is Gaza, which was occupied and governed by Egypt. Again, Egypt made zero attempt to create a Palestinian state during the time they occupied it.

As far as Jordan and Egypt were concerned the dark areas of map three were absolutely not Palestinian land; they considered these areas sovereign territory and governed them accordingly, offering the Arab Palestinians no civil rights. Did anyone protest that? The answer is no.

Israel took control of the West Bank from Jordan and Gaza from Egypt in a defensive move in the Six-Day War of 1967; the West Bank, Gaza and the Golan Heights, were all used by the Arabs as bases from which to attack Israel (the strategic importance of the West Bank, Gaza and the Golan Heights in the defence of Israel became even clearer in the 1973 conflict).

Israel pleaded with Jordan not to enter the war in 1967 but the king of Jordan ignored their plea and attacked. Had Jordan not done so, the West Bank would still be under Jordanian rule and the Arab Palestinians living there would have significantly less say in governing it than they do now. Likewise, had Egypt not attacked Israel, Gaza would still be under Egyptian rule and the Palestinians would still not have any say in governing it.

Map Four

Map four alleges to show what remains of Palestinian land today as a result of Israel's progressive illegal land grab.

Map four shows Gaza as Palestinian land following Israel's full withdrawal in 2005, resulting in Hamas taking control a year later. Gaza is shown slightly reduced when compared to map one not because Israel has stolen part of it, but because Egypt still controls parts of the strip from Rafah to the south.

Why does map four show the West Bank in such a reduced manner?

In 1995, as part of the Oslo Accords agreed between Israel and the Palestinian Authority in an attempt to stop the Arab terror attacks on Israeli citizens, the West Bank was divided into three administrative zones, A, B and C. Zone A is administered by the Palestinian Authority, zone C by Israel and zone B jointly by both the Palestinian Authority and Israel. The reality is that this arrangement gives the Palestinian Authority either full autonomy or shared control of a large area of the West Bank.

While admittedly this is not ideal for either Israel nor the Arabs living in the West Bank, two important factors need to be kept in mind. The first is why the West Bank had to be divided. It was divided as a way of putting an end to the deadly terror attacks being carried out on Israeli citizens. Israel would be delighted and relieved to hand the entire West Bank over to the Palestinian Authority if they would provide assurance of no further terror attacks. Sadly, that is not forthcoming.

Secondly, the current position of the West Bank still gives the Arabs living there significantly more autonomy than they had when it was annexed by Jordan.

These four maps are guilty of a further misrepresentation. As I have previously mentioned, map one dishonestly implies

Arabs were spread out and living in all the dark area. Anyone who has believed the lie of map one will naturally wonder how all those Arabs who previously lived across map one are now all crammed into the dark area of map four. The fact is they are not. In spite of over two million Arabs happily living in Israel as Israeli citizens, there is zero shading outside the dark areas of either Gaza or the part of the West Bank controlled solely by the Palestinian Authority to reflect this; it is also worth pointing out that the Arabs living in Israel have a significantly better quality of life than Arabs living in Arab controlled Gaza or the West Bank.